A CHILDREN'S ALMANAC OF WORDS AT PLAY

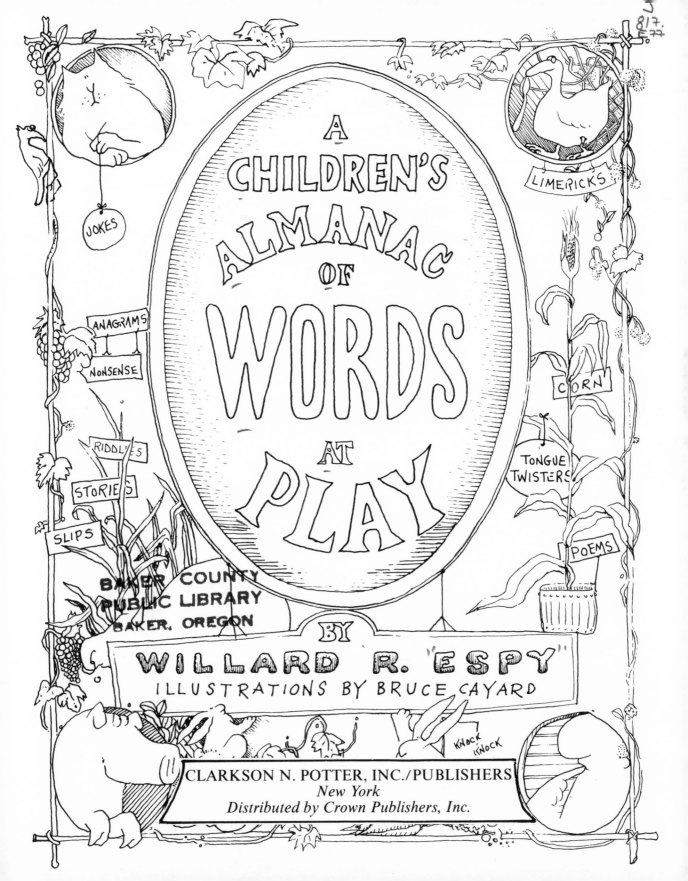

A CHILDREN'S ALMANAC OF WORDS AT PLAY

JOKES

LIMERICKS

ANAGRAMS

NONSENSE

CORN

RIDDLES

STORIES

TONGUE TWISTERS

SLIPS

POEMS

BY WILLARD R. ESPY

ILLUSTRATIONS BY BRUCE CAYARD

KNOCK KNOCK

CLARKSON N. POTTER, INC./PUBLISHERS
New York
Distributed by Crown Publishers, Inc.

Published by Clarkson N. Potter, Inc., One Park Avenue, New York, New York 10016, and simultaneously in Canada by General Publishing Company Limited

Manufactured in the United States of America

Library of Congress Cataloging in Publication Data

Espy, Willard R.
    A children's almanac of words at play.

    Includes index.
    Summary: An assortment of writings, including limericks, riddles, and puns, for each day of the year.
    1. Literary calendars. [1. Literary calendars]
I. Title.
PN6075.E8   818'.5407   82-7593
ISBN 0-517-54660-4   AACR2
ISBN 0-517-54666-3 (pbk.)

10 9 8 7 6 5 4 3 2 1

FIRST EDITION

Foreword

DEAR ALEXANDER, ELLIOTT, MEDORA, JEREMY, JOANNA, AND TAYLOR:

I do not know which me wrote this book. People are not the same at ten, say, as they are at twenty or thirty or sixty. How can I know which me I am when I don't know how old I am? I must be more than five, because I was five when I learned to tie my shoelaces in a double knot, and I have been tying my shoelaces in a double knot for a long time. And I can't be a hundred and ten yet, because I never met anyone who lived to be a hundred and ten. Somebody once told me that the way to tell my age was to count my teeth, but I think that is wrong. It might work for a newborn baby; it has no teeth, and is not even one year old. But a hundred-and-ten-year-old man probably would have no teeth either. Does that make him as young as a newborn baby?

Besides, I cannot count the teeth in my head two times in succession and get the same answer. I think they grow in and fall out faster than I can count. Or else I don't know when to stop counting. The highest number of teeth I have counted at one time is ninety-three, so almost certainly I am no older than that. My best guess is that I am somewhere between five and fifteen.

Anyhow, I know how old *you* are,* and that is what counts.

Love,

Pop

*These were the ages of my grandchildren when I began to prepare this book:
Alexander was twelve.
Elliott was ten.
Medora was eight.
Jeremy was seven.
Joanna was three.
Taylor was two.
Joanna and Taylor do not talk as often in the book as the other children do. That is because they are so young.

(If you are not, say, eight yet, some entries may not amuse you. Skip them. If you are ten, you won't want to do much skipping. And if you are going on for twelve I hope you will laugh very hard at everything.)

Acknowledgments

MY FIRST SOURCE of entries for *The Children's Almanac* was my own earlier books of wordplay. I then examined nearly a hundred children's books of poems, puzzles, jokes and riddles, many of which have overlapping entries. I drew heavily also on *Word Ways, The Journal of Recreational Linguistics.*

Wherever a poem is used without attribution, the name of the author is unknown, at least to me.

I owe special thanks for their contributions to Jane R. Barliss, William Cole, Hume R. Craft, Faith Eckler, William Engel, Darryl Francis, David Goldberg, Norman Hickman, Dotty Hillman, Richard Kostelanetz, A. F. G. Lewis, Christine Loya, Mildred Luton, Mary Ann Madden, Paul E. Manheim, Scot Morris, Louis Phillips, Mala Powers, Ruth Tepper, J. D. White, and Mary J. Youngquist.

Grateful acknowledgment is made to the following publishers and authors for permission to reprint or adapt material:

February 26 "Guess What?" by Leo Rosten. Reprinted by permission of the author.

February 29 "As Saint Patrick Goes Walking" from *The New Book of Days* by Eleanor Farjeon. Published by Oxford University Press. Reprinted by permission of David Higham Associates Limited.

March 11 "Sing Song" by Arnold Adoff from *Scribner Anthology for Young People,* edited by Anne Diven. Copyright © 1976 by Charles Scribner's Sons (New York: Charles Scribner's Sons, 1976). Reprinted with the permission of Charles Scribner's Sons.

March 24 "You Cannot Tell" from *The New Book of Days* by Eleanor Farjeon. Published by Oxford University Press. Reprinted by permission of David Higham Associates Limited.

Guarantee

THIS IS A MONEY-BACK GUARANTEE that you can get the answers to all the puzzles in this book. All you have to do is look in the back.

If you like a certain kind of puzzle, you'll find more of the same kind by looking in the Index at the back of the book.

You are supposed to read just as much of this book as you wish, no more. If an entry fails to amuse you, just skip.

January

1 January

JANUARY's name, of course,
Comes from JANUS,* god of doors.
JANUARY's gales affright;
Shut your doors and windows tight.

—W.R.E.

If your life began
In JAN
You will start to ebb
In FEB,
Eat a candy bar
In MAR,
Cut a lively caper
In APR,
Dance a roundelay
In MAY,
Sing a pretty tune
In JUN.

You will play the fool
In JUL;
Live high off the hog
In AUG;
You will be adept
In SEPT
But grow old and crocked
In OCT,
Huddle by the stove
In NOV.
And your life will cease
In DEC.

—W.R.E.

*Janus had two faces. One looked back, toward the past, and the other forward, toward the future.

2 January————————————

Once A-pun a Time

A pun is a word used for another word that sounds like it but has a different meaning.

Once a-pun a time, Alexander, Elliott, Jeremy, and Joanna visited for several weeks at the home of Medora and Taylor, their cousins. I was often there, too. One day I told Alexander, Elliott, Medora, and Jeremy (for Joanna and Taylor were still too young to play this game) that I would pay each of them a dime for a pun. But they wanted more than a dime, so each of them gave me *two* puns.

Alexander started by using *crime* when he meant *climb*.

"Monkeys crime trees," he said.

"*Trees* a crowd," said Elliott.

"The rooster made a loud noise when he *crowd*," said Jeremy.

"My *noise* is between my eyes," said Medora.

"*Eyes* are the opposite of nays," said Alexander.

"A horse *neighs*," said Elliott.

"A horse can have a colt," said Jeremy.

"I was *hoarse* last night," said Medora. "This morning I woke up with a *colt*."

3 January————————————

I glanced in a mirror in Deere,
And found that I looked rather queer:
   Two noses, three faces,
   Four jokers, five aces,
One eye, and the half of an ear.
          —W.R.E.

A bald-headed person named Twig
Once went for advice to a pig.
   Said the pig, "Make some snares,
   And catch a few hares,
And weave the hares into a wig."
          —W.R.E.

A yak from the hills of Iraq
Met a yak he had known awhile back.
   They went out to dine,
   And talked of lang syne—
Yak-ety, yak-ety, yak.
          —W.R.E.

I Know Where I'm Going

Your teacher might mark this poem with a big red X, because the first stanza says "who" twice when the right word is "whom." But the poem was written hundreds of years ago, and the woman talking was supposed to have been without schooling; her mistakes make me like the verse even better.

I know where I'm going.
I know who's going with me,
I know who I love,
But the dear knows who I'll marry.

I'll have stockings of silk,
Shoes of fine green leather,
Combs to buckle my braid,
And a ring for every finger.

Feather beds are soft,
Painted rooms are bonny;
But I'd leave them all
To go with my love, Johnny.

Some say he's dark,
I say he's bonny,
He's the flower of them all,
My handsome, coaxing Johnny.

I know where I'm going,
I know who's going with me,
I know who I love,
But the dear knows who I'll marry.

A PICTURE POEM

5 January

miniskirtminiskirt

miniskirtminiskirtmi

niskirtminiskirtminisk

irtminiskirtminiskirtmin

legleglegleglegleglegleglegleglegleg   legleglegleglegleglegleglegleglegleg

shoe   shoe

—ANTHONY MUNDY

ACCIDENTAL ENGLISH

6 January

After car accidents, the drivers are supposed to write out everything that happened so that their insurance companies can tell who was to blame. Sometimes the drivers are still in shock, and their reports don't make much sense. Those that follow are cross-my-heart-and-hope-to-die true; they were copied from insurance forms by my fifth cousin William, who is an honest man:

Coming home, I drove into the wrong house and collided with a tree I don't have.

A pedestrian hit me and went under my car.

The guy was all over the road; I had to swerve a number of times before I hit him.

I had been driving my car for forty years when I fell asleep at the wheel and had an accident.

I was sure the old fellow would never make it to the other side of the street when I struck him.

The pedestrian had no idea which direction to go, so I ran over him.

I was thrown from my car as it left the road. I was later found in a ditch by some stray cows.

The telephone pole was approaching fast. I attempted to swerve out of the way, when it struck the front of my car.

—WILLIAM G. ESPY

7 January ————————————————————

How Many Apples?

In magic tricks, the magician makes you think he is doing one thing, like stuffing a handkerchief into his thumb, when he is really doing something else. Riddles are a kind of word magic: The question is put so as to fool you, instead of helping you get the answer. The first three questions below are old-fashioned riddles, but the last two are different. After all, how can you know how many bones you have in your body unless someone tells you?

1. A farmer in Idaho has a beautiful plum tree. The main trunk has 24 branches, each branch has 12 boughs, each bough has 6 twigs and each twig bears 1 fruit. How many apples on the tree?

2. How do you pronounce VOLIX?

3. A rope ladder 12 feet long is hanging over the side of a ship. The rungs of the ladder are one foot apart, and the lowest rung is resting on the top of the ocean. The tide rises six inches an hour. How long will it take for the first four rungs of the ladder to be underwater?

4. A very fat woman and two very thin women have to cross a stream in a boat that can carry only 200 pounds. The fat woman weighs 200 pounds and the two very thin women each weigh 100 pounds. How can they cross?

5. When Alexander says to Elliott, "I'll break every bone in your body," how many bones is he talking about? 100? 200? 500? 1,000?

8 January————————————————————————

Sometimes words are put together to make amusing sounds rather than to make sense. Often two words are combined into one just for the rhyme or the echo. Most of this verse is made of words like that.

HOITY-TOITY

Hoity-toity, where is nanny?
There's some hanky-panky here.
Double trouble, frangipani,
Topsy-turvy, jiggledy-wiggledy,
Hugger-mugger, higgledy-piggledy,
Ragtag, claptrap, flip-flop, queer.
    REFRAIN: Beulah, set up one more beer.

Whippersnapper, rooty-tooty,
Helter-skelter, tutti-frutti;
Have a wingding, silly Billy,
Lick'ty-split, don't shally-shilly,
Nim'ny-pim'ny, willy-nilly,
Hocus-pocus, there's a dear.
    REFRAIN: Beulah, set up one more beer.

Hipp'ty-hopp'ty, hurry-scurry,
Mumbo jumbo, don't you worry;
Hurdy-gurdy plays by ear.
Pop's a jim-jam fuddy-duddy,
Namby-pamby is dear muddy;
Unc's a hunky-dory foola,
Granny, she does hula-hula . . .
Who's an eager beaver? *Beulah!*
    REFRAIN: Bring another round of beer!
                      —W.R.E.

WHERE
THOSE
WORDS
DIDN'T
COME
FROM

9 January————————————————————————

Bully *Is a Bully Word*

Some people think the word *bully*, meaning a person who abuses smaller and weaker people, comes from *bull*; bulls are said to chase boys and girls and make them climb trees. But it really comes from a Dutch word meaning sweetheart. The word changed to mean a good friend, a fine fellow. That is what Shakespeare meant by it when he had Pistol say in *Henry V,* speaking of the king, "From heartstring I love the lovely bully." Then good friends who gathered together in groups to beat up innocent passers-by began to call themselves bullies; and that is how the word took its present meaning.

The *bull* in *bulldog* does not come from *bull* either, although the dogs were once used to bait bulls. It comes from the shape of a bulldog's head— round, like a ball. *Ball* was *boule* in French; a bulldog is really a balldog.

The word *cheese* in "big cheese" (a big cheese is "big stuff") has nothing to do with the food; it is the way the English pronounced the Hindi word *chiz,* "thing."

Blindworms aren't blind, and they aren't worms; they are legless lizards.

Turkeys are native to North America, not Turkey; the ship that carried them just happened to stop in Turkey on the way to England.

You are probably the only one in your class who knows all this.

10 January————————————————— CROSSING JOKES

When Elliott was small, he was a towhead, and his hair stood out in spikes. It looked like unmowed hay. Now that he is ten years old, his hair is darker, and he brushes it hard, so that it lies down most of the time. When I met him in the yard this morning, though, it was standing in spikes again. That was because he was excited—he had just come across some new crossing jokes, and he couldn't wait to try them out.

"Cross a cowboy with a cook," he demanded of Jeremy, "and what do you get?"

"Someone who cooks cows?" asked Jeremy.

"No," said Elliott. "You get a Hopalong Casserole. Cross a zebra with an apeman, and what do you get?"

"I give up," said Jeremy.

"Tarzan stripes forever," said Elliott. "Cross Pinocchio with an employment agency, and what do you get?"

Jeremy shook his head.

"A nose job," said Elliott.

Then he went inside the house, and I heard his mother telling him to brush his hair.

11 January

Alligator, Beetle, Porcupine, Whale

The first letter of the first line in this verse is A; the first letter of the second line is B; and so on through the alphabet. The verse names 104 animals, birds, fish, and insects.

Alligator, beetle, porcupine, whale,
Bobolink, panther, dragonfly, snail,
Crocodile, monkey, buffalo, hare,
Dromedary, leopard, mud turtle, bear,
Elephant, badger, pelican, ox,
Flying fish, reindeer, anaconda, fox,
Guinea pig, dolphin, antelope, goose,
Hummingbird, weasel, pickerel, moose,
Ibex, rhinoceros, owl, kangaroo,
Jackal, opossum, toad, cockatoo,
Kingfisher, peacock, anteater, bat,
Lizard, ichneumon, honeybee, rat,
Mockingbird, camel, grasshopper, mouse,
Nightingale, spider, cuttlefish, grouse,
Ocelot, pheasant, wolverine, auk,
Periwinkle, ermine, katydid, hawk,
Quail, hippopotamus, armadillo, moth,
Rattlesnake, lion, woodpecker, sloth,
Salamander, goldfinch, angleworm, dog,
Tiger, flamingo, scorpion, frog,
Unicorn, ostrich, nautilus, mole,
Viper, gorilla, basilisk, sole,
Whippoorwill, beaver, centipede, fawn,
Xeme, canary, polliwog, swan,
Yellowhammer, eagle, hyena, lark,
Zebra, chameleon, butterfly, shark.

An epitaph is an inscription on a tombstone. Those below were carved many years ago. A tombstone seems an odd place for a joke.

ON ANN MANN

Here lies Ann Mann;
She lived an old maid
But died an old Mann.

ON OWEN MOORE

Owen Moore:
Gone away
Owin' More
Than he could pay.

ON MARY WEARY, HOUSEWIFE

Dere friends I am going
Where washing ain't done
Or cooking or sewing;
Don't mourn for me now
Or weep for me never:
For I go to do nothing
Forever and ever.

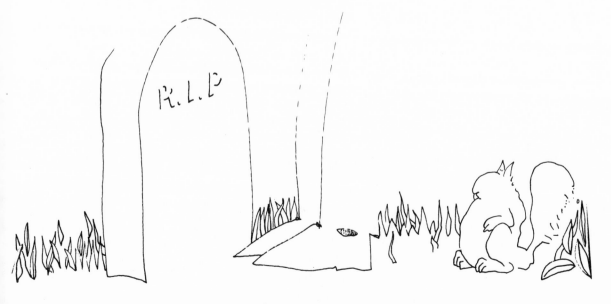

13 January

I know *you* aren't superstitious. You don't stay in bed on Friday the Thirteenth. You walk under a ladder without thinking twice about it. (Perhaps you should think twice though; a bucket of paint may fall on your head.)

But not everybody is as clever as you. Why, there may be children in your own class who believe superstitions like these:

That part of your soul is caught in a picture of you. Primitive people sometimes refuse to have their photograph taken, for fear that it can be used to bewitch them.

That a pinch of salt thrown over the left shoulder will protect you from bad luck. It is supposed to keep the devil at a distance. And if salt is spilled, there will be a quarrel.

That bubbles in coffee mean money, while bubbles in a teacup mean visitors are coming. (A sudden itch, or silverware falling to the floor, also is a sign of visitors.)

That if your ears burn, someone is talking about you.

That if you step on a crack, you will fail at something you are trying to do.

That it is bad luck to break a mirror, postpone a wedding, or open an umbrella indoors. (Or, for that matter, to turn back from a journey, stub a toe, wear clothes inside out, meet a black cat or funeral procession, sit on a table, or leave a house through a window.)

That it is good luck to possess a rabbit's foot or horseshoe, find a four-leaf clover, or pick up a pin.

That fairies, elves, and sprites help human beings, while gnomes and goblins are full of mischief, causing milk to sour and even stealing babies and leaving changelings in their place.

Of course you don't believe such nonsense. Just to make sure that nothing bad happens, though, it might be a good idea to knock on wood.

14 January

Little Willie was constantly involved in disasters so very gory that verses written about them seem funny instead of horrible. "Sick" verses like the two below are called Little Willies even when Little Willie does not appear in them.

> Willie built a guillotine,
> Tried it out on sister Jean.

Said mother as she got the mop,
"These messy games have got to stop!"
—WILLIAM ENGELS

Father heard his children scream,
So he threw them in the stream,
Saying, as he drowned the third,
"Children should be seen, not heard!"
—HARRY GRAHAM

15 January——————————————————— KNOCK KNOCKS

1. Knock knock.
   Who's there?
   Adolf.
   Adolf who?
   Adolf ball hit me,
   dat's why I talk dis way.

2. Knock knock,
   Who's there?
   Debbie.
   Debbie who?
   Debbie stung me.

3. Knock knock.
   Who's there?
   Robin.
   Robin who?
   Robin you, so hand over your dough.

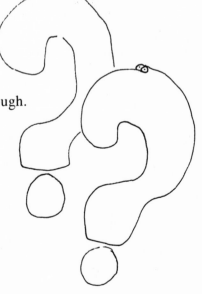

4. Knock knock.
   Who's there?
   Wendy.
   Wendy who?
   Wendy today; cloudy tomorrow.

5. Knock knock.
   Who's there?
   Harry.
   Harry who?
   Harry up and answer the door.

16 January———————————————

This is the way things are outdoors in January:

> Oh, what a blamed uncertain thing
> This pesky weather is:
> It blew and blew and then it snew,
> And now, by jing, it friz!
>
> ———•———
>
> I sneezed a sneeze into the air,
> It fell to earth I knew not where;
> But hard and cold were the looks of those
> In whose vicinity I snooze.

17 January———————————————

In this game, you are supposed to replace one letter of a word with another letter, making a new word. Keep changing them until you have the word you want. Here is how it is done:

1. Turn *black* into *white* in seven moves.
   Black, brack, brace, trace, trice, trite, write, white
2. Turn *dog* into *cat* in three moves.
   Dog, dot, cot, cat or *dog, cog, cot, cat*

Now try the six word-changes below.

3. Turn *dusk* through *dark* into *dawn* in seven moves.
4. Turn *east* into *west* in three moves.
5. Turn *hate* into *love* in three moves.
6. Turn *heat* into *fire* in five moves.
7. Turn *lead* into *gold* in three moves.
8. Turn *lion* into *bear* in five moves.

DOWN GOES EZRA

For a lark,
For a prank,
Ezra Clark
Walked a plank.
These bubbles mark
   o
   o
   o
   o
   o
  Where Ezra sank.

Only Seven Times Only

Put *only* in the first blank space in the sentence below. Then move it from the first space to the second, then from the second to the third, and so on. With each shift of position, the sentence will change its meaning:*

  —— I —— hit —— him —— in
the —— eye —— yesterday ——.

1. —— I hit him in the eye yesterday.
2. I —— hit him in the eye yesterday.
3. I hit —— him in the eye yesterday.
4. I hit him in —— the eye yesterday.
5. I hit him in the —— eye yesterday.
6. I hit him in the eye —— yesterday.
7. I hit him in the eye yesterday ——.

*Ernest Brennecke made up the sentence.

20 January

I Sawyer Saw. Does That Make Me a Sawyer?

If you grant that:
A man sawing wood in the woods is a sawyer
While a second man, practicing law, is a lawyer

It follows that:
A crab has a claw, so a crab is a clawyer;
The rat that is gnawing my cheese is a gnawyer;
A crow, since it caws, is no crow but a cawyer.

Let us now apply this logic to you and yours:
If you suck up your tea with a straw, you're a strawyer;
If your gem has a flaw, it's no gem but a flawyer;
If your yawl starts to yaw, then your yawl is a yawyer;
If your baby Charles baws, he must be a Charles Boyer.*

Which leads to this doleful conclusion:
If these helpful lines stick in your craw, you're a crawyer.
Do I hear you say pshaw? Pshaw to you too, you pshawyer.

—W.R.E.

*Charles Boyer was a famous motion picture actor.

21 January

Chiffchaff

Alexander was born in Washington, and learned to talk in Bolivia. Elliott was born in Bolivia, and learned to talk in Uganda. Jeremy was born in Uganda, and learned to talk in Brazil. (You see, their father was a U. S. foreign service officer.) So they know that sounds seem to change from one language to another. Take, for instance, the call of the chiffchaff, a European warbler. Here is the way it comes out in various languages:

English: chiff, chaff, chiff, chiff, chaff
Finnish: til, tal, til, til, tal
German: zilp, zalp, zilp, zilp, zalp
French: tyip, tsyep, tyip, tyip, tsyep
Dutch: tjif, tjaf, tjif, tjif, tjaf

Swedish: tji, tju, tji, tji, tju
Spanish: sib, sab, sib, sib, sab
Italian: ciff, ciaff, ciff, ciff, ciaff
Icelandic: tsjiff, tsjaff, tsjiff, tsjiff, tsjaff
Danish: tjif, tjaf, tjif, tjif, tjaf

Do Americans really hear sounds differently from, say, the Dutch? Or is it that they have different spellings for the same sound? Or both? I don't think anybody is quite sure. We do know, though, that a chiffchaff doesn't really make consonant sounds like *ch* and *t* and *z* and *ty* at all. It just makes vowel sounds, and our minds fill in the consonants.

22 January———————————

Ten Animals

The cat is the only domestic animal not mentioned in the Bible. Clearly, the cat never entered heaven. Indeed, tradition says only ten animals did. They are listed here:

> Ten animals, and ten alone
>   Were raised to Paradise—
> The Gate is closed to Cuttlefish,
>   The Gate is closed to Flies;
>
> The Crabs and Worms must stay outside,
>   The Geese and Chimpanzees—
> But Kratim's there (the Dog who speaks).
>   He prays along with these:
>
> The Calf of Abraham; the Ant
>   Of Solomon, in prayer
> With Sheba's Cuckoo; Moses' Ox;
>   Muhammad's milk-white Mare.
>
> There Ram of Isaac, Jonah's Whale
>   And Saleh's Camel raise
> Their voices to their risen Lord
>   With Balaam's Ass . . . who brays.
>   —W.R.E.

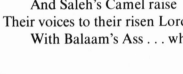

23 January

No Ephs or Cays

If you were a printer, and found that the letters *f* and *k* had disappeared from your supply of type, how would you solve the problem? You would substitute other letters that have the same sounds. At least that is what the *Rocky Mountain Cyclone* printer did in the following passage:*

We begin the publication of the *Roccay Mountain Cyclone* with some phew diphphiculties. The type phounders phrom whom we bought our outphit phor this printing ophphice phailed to supply us with any ephs or cays, and it will be phour to phive weex bephore we can get any. The mistaque was not phound out till a day or two ago. We have ordered the missing letters, and will have to get along without them till they come. We don't lique the loox ov this variety ov spelling any better than our readers, but mistaques will happen in the best regulated phamilies, and iph the ephs and cays and xs and qs hold out, we shall ceep (sound the c hard) the *Cyclone* whirling, aphter a phashion, till the letters arrive. It is no joque to us—it is a serious aphphair.

*As reprinted in *The Inland Printer*, January 1887.

24 January

Unlucky Friday

My friend Scot Morris collects surprising facts. I know the statements below are true, because Scot told me so.

To cure British sailors of their silly, superstitious fear of Fridays, the British government laid the keel of a new ship on a Friday, launched her on a Friday, named her H.M.S. *Friday,* and sent her on her first voyage on a Friday. Neither the ship nor her crew was ever seen again.

The blood vessels in a blue whale are so large that a fully grown trout could swim comfortably through the major arteries and veins.

The slipper-shelled snail, whose Latin name is *C. fornitica,* is a male when born, but turns female as it grows up.

When Ounce Is Spelled Oz.

If the abbreviation *oz.* is pronounced "ounce," why not spell all "ounce" sounds oz.? Here is the way it would work:

> A girl who weighed many an oz.
> Used language I dare not pronoz.
> When a fellow unkind
> Pulled her chair out behind
> Just to see (so he said) if she'd boz.

Just as *oz.* is pronounced "ounce," so *Co.* is pronounced "company." That being so, figured Mark Twain, *tho.* would be pronounced "thump any," and *do.* would be pronounced "dump any." And he proceeded to write this limerick:

> A man hired by John Smith and Co.
> Loudly declared he would tho.
> Man that he saw
> Dumping dirt near his store.
> The drivers, therefore, didn't do.
> —MARK TWAIN

The Golden Arm

The best time to tell this story is when the lights are out. Alexander likes to tell it before a fire when he has a friend sleeping over.

An old man lost his arm, and replaced it with an arm of gold. Then he died.

His widow said, "If I can get that golden arm, I will be rich. I will not need to worry about Social Security."

So one night, when the wind was howling and clouds hid the moon, she slipped into the graveyard and dug up her husband's body and took away the arm.

When she returned home, she heard a distant voice:

"Whoooo stole my golden arm? Whoooo stole my golden arm?"

She locked the doors. She locked the windows. She got into bed and pulled the blankets over her head.

But the voice came closer and closer:

"Whoooo stole my golden arm? Whoooo stole my golden arm?"

She heard the downstairs door open. She heard footsteps coming up the stairs. She heard the door to her bedroom open. Then, through the blankets, she heard the voice again, moaning right next to her ear:

"Whoooo stole my golden arm? Whoooo? Whoooo?"

[At this point, Alexander pauses. Then he grabs Medora, or whoever is next to him, and shouts:]

"YOU DID!"

JOKES

27 January————————————————

Tomfooleries

Most jokes, riddles, and puns have been around for a long time; we usually do not discover new ones; we simply revive the old ones. But some people are better at reviving than others. One of the best is Alvin Schwartz, who wrote *Tomfoolery.* Here are some tomfooleries that Jeremy likes:

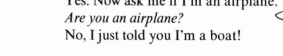

Take any number.
Add ten.
Subtract three.
Now close your eyes.
Dark, isn't it?

I knew a fellow who had snew in his blood.
What's snew?
Not much with me. What's new with you?

I bet I can jump across the street.
I bet you can't.
(Walk across the street and jump.)

Ask me if I'm a boat.
Are you a boat?
Yes. Now ask me if I'm an airplane.
Are you an airplane?
No, I just told you I'm a boat!

The post office correctly delivered a letter that bore only this inscription:

> WOOD
> JOHN
> MASS

Some clever postman figured that it was a code meaning JOHN *UNDER* WOOD *AND OVER,* MASS.

> John Underwood
> Andover, Mass.

This kind of riddle, made of pictures or words that suggest the sounds of the syllables to be guessed, is called a *rebus.* See if you can solve the five rebuses below.

1.
    ADO
ADO ADO
   O
ADO ADO
  ADO

2.   WORLAMEN

3.   E
    M
    A
    R
    F

4.   ONALLE

5.   M E
    A L

—MARY J. YOUNGQUIST

> Old Mother Hubbard
> Went to the cupboard
> To get her poor dog a bone.
> When she got there,
> The cupboard was bare.
> and she said: O I C U R M T !

30 January

It's Getting Warmer

Elliott tells this story, and laughs hard at the end, whether anybody else laughs or not:

> My history teacher says that Poland and Russia have been at war with each other off and on for hundreds of years. An old Pole had a farm right on the border. When the Russians were winning, his land was in Russia. When the Poles were winning, his land was in Poland. One day a Polish general came to tell him that the war was over, and the Poles had won. "From now on," he said, "your farm will always be Polish territory." "Thank God," said the old man. "Now no more of those terrible Russian winters."

31 January

Say, Who Will Write a Pun My Stone?

"On January 31, 1902," I said, "they hanged Lum You."

"Who was Lum You?" asked Elliott.

"He was a Chinese laborer in Pacific County, Washington, where I lived when I was a boy."

"Pop," said Jeremy, "were you already alive in 1902?"

"I was not. But Lum You was. He shot a man named Oscar Bloom. Most of the citizens thought Oscar Bloom needed shooting. After a jury had brought in a conviction the sheriff left Lum You's jail door open so that he could escape. But he gave himself up, and they had to hang him. I have one of the cards inviting people to the hanging."

Here is the card:

M Chris Davis
You are respectfully invited to be present
at the execution of
LUM YOU
Friday, January 31, 1902, at the Pacific County Court
House at 9:00 o'clock a. m.
Present this Card
Not Transferable   Sheriff

"Poor Lum You," said Medora.

"No one seems to know just where he was buried," I said. "I wish I could find out. I'd like to raise money for a headstone."

"What would it say?" asked Alexander.

I wrote the legend on a piece of wrapping paper:

I LUM YOU (1873–1902).

WHY YOU NO LUM ME?

February

1 February

FEBRUARY

Snow is getting boring. I grow very
Sick of wintertime by FEBRUARY.

—W.R.E.

What is the name of the little trench that separates your nose from your upper lip? I used to know. Then I forgot, and wrote in a book:

Between my nose and upper lip
There runs a cleft; a trough; a slip;
A runnel; furrow; gutter; split.
I wish I knew the name for it.

Readers promptly told me the name was *philtrum.* Nowadays I sing:

I have a little philtrum
Wherein my spilltrum flows
When I am feeling illtrum
And runny at the nose.

Colds are common this month, and your philtrum is likely to be particularly busy.

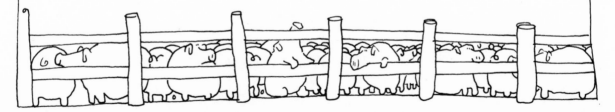

2 February——————————————————————

- Why is a cow's tail like the bosom of a swan?
  Because it grows down.

- What question can never be answered "Yes"?
  "Are you asleep?"

- Why is a dog biting its tail like a good manager?
  Because it makes both ends meet.

- Why do hens always lay eggs in the daytime?
  Because at night they become roosters.

- The woods are two miles across. How far can you go into them?
  One mile. After that, you are going out.

- What did one strawberry say to the other?
  If you weren't so fresh, we wouldn't be in this jam.

- What did one eye say to the other?
  There's something between us that smells.

3 February——————————————————————

Spanker

Large lively ladies leap in lyrical elation;
Lick their lips and laugh aloud—and that's *alliteration*!

—W.R.E.

And so it is, because alliteration is the use of the same sound to start several words in a row. *Sing a song of sixpence,* for instance. Or this advertisement of an English horse sale in 1829:

Saturday, the Sixteenth September next, will be sold, or set up for sale, at Skibbereen:

A strong, staunch, steady, sound, stout, safe, sinewy, serviceable, strapping, supple, swift, smart, sightly, sprightly, spirited, sturdy, shining, sure-footed, sleek, smooth, spunky, well-skinned, sized and shaped sorrel steed, of superlative symmetry, styled SPANKER; with small star and snip, square-sided, slender-shouldered, sharp-sighted, and steps singularly stately; free from strain, spavin, spasms, stringhalt, staggers, strangles, surfeit, seams, strumous swellings, scratches, splint, squint, scurf, sores, scattering, shuffling, shambling gait, or sickness of any sort. He is neither stiff-mouthed, shabby-coated, sinew-shrunk, saddle-backed, shell-toothed, skin-scabbed, short-winded, splay-footed, nor shoulder-slipped; and is sound in the sword point and stifle joint. . . . His selling price is sixty-seven pounds, sixteen shillings, and sixpence sterling.

Speaking of the letter *s:* It begins at least 37,000 words—more than any other letter. And it combines with every other letter except *x* and *b*.

4 February ————————————————————————

Alexander's Favorite Counting-out Rhymes

Up the ladder, down the ladder,
See the monkeys chew tobacco.
How many ounces did they chew?
Shut your eyes and think.
—*Six.*
One, two, three, four, five, six,
And out you must go for saying so.

Mickey Mouse bought a house,
What color did he paint it?
Shut your eyes and think.
—*Red.*
R-E-D spells red,
And out you must go for saying so,
With a clip across your ear hole.

My mother and your mother
Were hanging out the clothes,
My mother gave your mother
A punch on the nose.
What color was the blood?
Shut your eyes and think.
—*Blue.*
B-L-U-E spells blue, and out you go
With a whopping clout upon your big nose.

5 February————————————————————

I Fooled You!

"I know what you're going to say next," said Medora.

"What?" asked Jeremy.

"*That's* what!" said Medora.

"Put your finger to your head and give the abbreviation for mountain," said Medora.

"I won't," said Jeremy. "You are playing a trick."

"Oh, go ahead," said Medora.

"M-o-u-n-t," said Jeremy, pointing with his finger.

"That's *wrong*! It's *not* the abbreviation for mountain!"

"Then what is?"

"MT is the abbreviation for mountain. You are supposed to point at your head like *this,* and say MT!"

"Your head's empty!" shouted Jeremy.

"I bet I can make you say 'black,' " said Medora.

"I bet you can't," said Jeremy.

"What color is the American flag?"

"Red, white, and blue."

"See, I told you I could make you say 'blue.' "

"No, you said I'd say 'black.' "

"You just did. Ya, ya!" said Medora.

6 February————————————————————

Diamrab

In back slang, words are spelled and pronounced backward. Man backward is *nam;* curious is *suoiruc;* boy is *yob.*

This verse is based on back slang. How would it read in plain English?

A *diamrab* fell in love
And wed her *tseug.*
Of all earth's *nerdlihc*
Theirs were the *tse.*

—W.R.E.

7 February————————————————

Madam, I'm Adam

Alexander likes to play games like tennis and softball, but he particularly likes to play soccer. He has a soccer ball that he carries around in his arms as if it were a baby; today, back from a soccer match, he paused on his way to the bathroom for a shower when he saw me sitting and reading a book.

"Well, we won, Pop," he said, "and I scored twice."

"That's great," I said. "But Alexander, don't you think you should do something besides sports?"

"Oh, I do," he said. "I read. I read a lot."

I really knew that, of course. "What are you reading now, Alex?" I asked him.

"I am learning about palindromes. They are sentences that say the same thing whether they are written forward or backward. Like 'Madam, I'm Adam.' That's what Adam said the first time he met Eve. And 'A man, a plan, a canal. Panama.' That was about the man who built the Panama Canal."

"His name was Major Goethals," I said.

"Oh. And then there is, 'Was it a bar or a bat I saw?' And, 'He goddam mad dog, eh?' "

"Wait a minute. That last one is by James Thurber, who was a very funny writer, but he spelled *goddam* without the *n* at the end, so he cheated, and besides I don't want you going around swearing."

"You know I never swear, Pop," said Alexander.

(But he does sometimes, when he thinks the old folks can't hear.)

8 February————————————————

The abbreviation of Illinois is *Ill.*; *ill* means *sick*. Going by their abbreviations, give the names of these states:

1. The cleanest
2. The most seaworthy
3. The most fatherly
4. The most personal
5. The most surprised
6. The most professional
7. The most unmarried
8. The most Catholic
9. The highest numbered
10. The most Islamic
11. The best writer
12. The most shady

9 February

I Said, "This Horse, Sir"

English grammar has many rules, and many exceptions. If you try to make the past of one verb the same as the past of another one, you may get into trouble like this:

> I said, "This horse, sir, will you shoe?"
> And soon the horse was shod;
> I said, "This deed, sir, will you do?"
> And soon the deed was dod.
> I said, "This stick, sir, will you break?"
> At once the stick he broke;
> I said, "This coat, sir, will you make?"
> And soon the coat he moke.

10 February

Tootling in Tokyo

A computer, programmed to translate English into Russian and back into English, was given the expression "Out of sight, out of mind." The computer whirred. What came out? "Invisible insanity."

Translating is a tricky business. Here is how the Japanese in Tokyo translated traffic rules for the benefit of English-speaking drivers:

> When a passenger of the foot heave in sight, tootle the horn, trumpet at him melodiously at first, but if he still obstacles your passage, tootle him with vigor, express by mouth the warning Hi, hi! Beware the wandering horse that he shall not take fright as you pass him by. Do not explode the exhaust box at him. Go soothingly by. Give big space to the festive dog that shall sport in the roadway. Go soothingly in the grease-mud as there lurks the skid-demon. Avoid the entanglement of the dog with your wheel spokes. Press the braking of the foot as you roll around the corner to save collapse and tie-up.

11 February—————————————————

Medora through the Needle's Eye

Medora was trying to thread a needle. It is hard to fit the thread into the tiny hole, and Medora had closed one eye to see better with the other when a curious thing happened.

She fell through the eye of the needle.

She went through head first; and because she had been doing gymnastics at school, she landed on her hands, turned two somersaults, and ended standing up. She was in a springy meadow.

It was springy because the ground was springy under her feet. It was springy because flowers were bursting from their buds all over.

She said to herself, "I have gone through a fall; but now the fall is over, and the spring has come."

Then she wondered aloud, "But whatever happened to the winter?"

A turtle beside her said,

We have ter choose—
Ter win; ter lose;
I know that *some* er
Fond of summer,
But I have caught 'em
In the autumn,
Watched 'em splinter
In the winter,
Heard 'em sing
In the spring.
Every season
Has its reason.

"Who are some?" asked Medora.

"Some is the sum of several," said the turtle. "The sum of some is some more."

"You don't talk as well as the animals do in *Alice in Wonderland,*" said Medora.

"I know," said the turtle sadly, and suddenly disappeared into its shell. At the same moment, Medora heard her mother calling. She must have found her way out through the eye of the needle, because she answered her mother, and she certainly is here now.

12 February———————————————

A young man at Oxford University was sitting on his bed one day, pulling on his sox, when he thought of this verse:

> When Alexander Pope
> Accidentally trod on the soap,
> And came down on the back of his head—
> Never mind what he said.

The name of this young man was Eric Clerihew Bentley, and the four-line verse form he invented—which makes a comment on a famous person, without much regard for meter—is called a *clerihew,* after his middle name. Mr. Bentley wrote hundreds of clerihews, and other writers have been imitating him ever since.

This one is about a famous home-run hitter named Babe Ruth, who was at bat with two strikes against him. When the pitcher was winding up for the next pitch, Babe Ruth pointed to the place where he was going to hit the ball for a home run. And that is where he did hit it:

> Babe Ruth
> Generally told the truth.
> When he pointed over the wall
> That's where he hit the ball.
>
> —W. R. E.

Clerihews are supposed to be funny; everyone is entitled to pick his own favorites. Here are two that I like:

> Alfred, Lord Tennyson
> Lived upon venison;
> Not cheap, I fear,
> Because venison's deer.
>
> —E. C. BENTLEY

> Al Capone
> Did not work alone.
> He used a gang
> To go bang, bang, bang.
>
> —LOUIS PHILLIPS

(Al Capone was a gangster who bootlegged liquor back in the 1920s, when selling liquor was against the law. He was a wicked man, and his lieutenants killed many people. But the government could not prove that *he* had actually killed anyone; when he was finally sent to prison, it was for failing to pay his income taxes.)

13 February —————————————

A School of Fish

A foreigner looking at a picture of a number of vessels said, "See what a flock of ships." He was told that a flock of ships was called a fleet, and that a fleet of sheep was called a flock. And it was added, for his guidance in mastering the intricacies of our language, that a flock of girls is called a bevy, that a bevy of wolves is called a pack, and a pack of thieves is called a gang, and that a gang of angels is called a host, and that a host of porpoises is called a shoal. . . .

—C. C. BOMBAUGH

Words describing specialized groups of people, animals, or things are called *collective nouns:* a plague of locusts, a brood of hens, a wedge of swans. Collective nouns often suit the thing they describe: locusts *are* a plague, hens *do* brood, flying swans *do* make a wedge.

Here are nine collective nouns that play with words:

A *riot* of students • A *peck* of kisses • A *mine* of egotists • A *host* of parasites • A *range* of ovens • A *furrow* of brows • A *lot* of realtors • A *wagon* of teetotalers.

—MARY ANN MADDEN's puzzle page in *New York* magazine

Why not put together some collective nouns of your own?

14 February

Engine, engine number nine,
Will you be my valentine?

—W.R.E.

This is the legend of how St. Valentine's Day began.

When the Roman emperor Claudius II needed soldiers, he made a law against marrying because he felt that marriage made men want to stay home instead of fighting wars.

Now, a kindly priest named Valentine, seeing the love of young couples, married some secretly. But he was discovered and condemned to death.

Even in prison, Valentine showed his love for everyone. His jailer had a young daughter who was blind. And by a miracle, Valentine restored her sight. Just before his death, on February 14, he sent her a farewell message signed "From your Valentine."

Now, February 14 fell in the midst of a Roman festival called the Lupercalia. When Christianity became the religion of Rome, this joyous day was changed to St. Valentine's Day, in honor of the saint who gave his life to help lovers.

—MALA POWERS

There are many other legends about how Valentine's Day started, and no one knows for sure whether any of them are true. But we do know it is a good day for knock knocks like this:

Knock knock.
Who's there?
Karen.
Karen who?
Karen for you.

VALENTINE'S DAY

My love is like a cabbage
Divided into two;
The leaves I give to others,
But the heart I give to you.

I LOVE YOU

I love you, I love you,
I love you divine.
Please give me your bubble gum,
You're sitting on mine.

15 February———————————

Limey

There is a disease called scurvy that develops from lack of vitamin C. Most vitamin C comes from fruit, which in the days before refrigeration would not last on long sea voyages. Without vitamin C to protect them, sailors often fell victim to scurvy. They would grow very weak; their gums would bleed, and they would even bleed under the skin.

Then the British navy discovered that lime juice is rich in vitamin C—and lime juice lasts indefinitely without refrigeration. So the navy ordered regular rations of lime juice for its sailors. The juice made them the healthiest sailors on the high seas. It also gave them the name by which the British are now known all over the world—"limeys."

16 February———————————

Spoken like a Native

These are the names of a number of countries and cities as pronounced by their inhabitants. Can you recognize them?

1. Pyee-Daung-Su Myanma Nainggan-Daw
2. Sri Lanka
3. Chung-hua Mink-kuo
4. Chung-hua Jen-min Kung-ho Kuo
5. Po
6. Vasileon Tis Ellados
7. Lydveldid Island
8. Keshvare Shahanshahiyeiran
9. Daehan-Minkuk
10. Choson Minchu-Chui Inmin Konghwaguk

—BOB CONSIDINE

17 February————————————————

THE LITTLE ALPHABET BOOK

Aye, bee	Pea
Seedy,	Queue are
E, F, Gee!	Ess tea
H, eye,	You Vee
Jay & Kaye,	Double ewe
Ell,	Ex, why?
M,	Z.
N owe	—LOUIS PHILLIPS

18 February————————————————

In a Tom Swifty, somebody says something, and the word for the way he says it is a pun on what he says. (This may sound confusing at first, but you will catch on right away.) These Tom Swifties are from a crossword puzzle in the *New York Times*:

"Young M.D.," said Tom *intern*ally.
"Gold leaf," said Tom *guilt*ily.
"Shirtwaist," said Tom *blows*ily.
"Maid's night off," said Tom *helpless*ly.
"Pass me the cards," said Tom *ideal*ly.
"Zero," said Tom *naught*ily.
". . . and lose a few," said Tom *winsome*ly.
"X's and . . ." said Tom *wise*ly.
"I bequeath," said Tom *willing*ly.
"Just *Newsweek*," said Tom *timeless*ly.

19 February————————————————

I'd Like to Be a Corsican

Napoleon Bonaparte was born in Corsica, an island off Italy. I read a travel article in a magazine that said every man living in Corsica today thinks he could be a Napoleon too, if only he had a chance. *You* could be Napoleon— if only you were a Corsican:

I'd like to be a Corsican,
A coarsey, horsey Corsican,
And do the deeds a Corsican,
Or even those his horsican,
    His horsican, his horsican.

When weary grows the Corsican
Of wedded intercoursican
Arrange a quick divorcican
And trot off on his horsican,
    His horsican, his horsican.

With oaths and curses coarsican
Rob boys and girls by forcican
And if his throat grows hoarsican
Tap out his oaths in Morsican,
    In Morsican, in Morsican.

The Corsican, of Corsican
Take any course, that Corsican,
Of Corsican, of Corsican,
Of course, of course, of Corsican . . .
I'd like to be a Corsican.
                    —W.R.E.

20 February —————————————————— TONGUE TWISTERS

ELLIOTT: You can't repeat these words three times fast without mixing them up.

MEDORA: What words?

ELLIOTT: Red leather, yellow leather.

MEDORA (quickly): Red leather, yellow leather, red letter, yellow letter, red—I give up. Here is one for you: say twice, fast, "The clothes moth's mouth's closed."

ELLIOTT: I can't.

MEDORA: You see?

JUMBLE JINGLE

Pick up a stick up,
    A stick up now pick;
Let me hear you say that
    Nine times, *quick!*
—LAURA E. RICHARDS

THREE-MONTH TRUCE BEGINS (newspaper headline)

If a three-month truce is a truce in truth,
Is the truth of a truce in truth a three-month
    truce?

—W.R.E.

**MALA-
PROPISMS**

21 February

Death to Hitchhikers

"I demand the death penalty for hitchhikers!" shouted Senator Strom Thurmond. But of course he did not mean *hitchhikers,* who thumb car rides; he meant *highjackers,* who seize airplanes by force in mid-flight. He had used a word that sounded a little like the one he wanted, but had an entirely different meaning. This kind of unintended slip is known as a *malapropism,* after Mrs. Malaprop, a character in Richard Sheridan's play *The Rivals,* who was famous for confusing words that way.

The italic word in each sentence below is a malapropism.

What would the right word be in each of these sentences?

1. The Beatles started a *resolution* in popular music.
2. I was so surprised you could have knocked me over with a *fender.*
3. He was a wealthy *typhoon.*
4. Mr. Poindexter is a *busy-buggy.*
5. He treats me like the dirt *on* his feet.
6. My sister uses *massacre* on her eyes.
7. We took the *alligator* to the top of the Empire State Building.
8. The doctor used *biceps* to deliver the baby.

I often pause and wonder
 At fate's peculiar ways,
For nearly all our famous men
 Were born on holidays.

I Cannot Tell a Lie (to Pop)

"I cannot tell a lie—I did it," said George Washington when his father accused him of cutting down a cherry tree. The verse below begins with the first line of a poem by Joyce Kilmer about trees; but the rest, as you see, is about lying.

"I think that I shall never see,"
Said Washington, "a cherry tree,
However nice it is to chop,
That justifies a lie to Pop."
But later on, without a qualm,
He lied about the tree to Mom.
       —W.R.E.

Pedigree, Sincere

When the French wished to show how they were connected with some distant ancestor, they used a three-line symbol to indicate the descent from generation to generation. The symbol ( ) looked like the track of a crane, so they called it *pie de grue*—"crane's foot." In English, the word changed from *pie de grue* to *pedigree.* Your family tree is your pedigree—the foot of a crane.

Dishonest marble cutters in ancient Rome rubbed wax over the pillars and blocks they were selling, to hide cracks. The Roman Senate tried to stop this cheating by passing a law saying that all marble bought by the government must be wax-free, which in Latin is *sine cera. Sine cera* came to mean "without deception—honest." And *sincere* means "honest" to this day.

24 February

BULLFROG COMMUNIQUÉ

I know a pond where frogs repeat / the water's depth, but not in feet / or yards or inches. Here's the way / they issue a communiqué:

A croaky treble close to shore
repeats his findings o'er and o'er,
ankle deep . . . ankle deep . . . ankle deep,
and farther out a baritone
reports from his official zone,
Knee Deep . . . Knee Deep . . . Knee Deep,
and way out in the deepest place
a daddy frog's bull fiddle bass,
BELLY DEEP . . . BELLY DEEP . . . BELLY DEEP.
I waded through that pond one night
and, bless my soul, the frogs are right—
ankle deep
   Knee Deep
      BELLY DEEP.

—MILDRED LUTON

25 February

I knocked on Elliott's door to suggest that we go fishing, but he said:

"Sorry, Pop; I am thinking. I have to write a composition for my English class."

I said, "Elliott, you think too much. Mrs. Edward Craster wrote about an unfortunate thing that happened to a centipede from thinking too much. It went like this":

The centipede was happy quite
   Until a toad in fun
Said, "Pray, which leg goes after which?"
   That worked her mind to such a pitch
She lay distracted in the ditch
   Considering how to run.

"I'm no centipede," said Elliott.

"Maybe you're more of a water beetle. Hillaire Belloc said a water beetle can think too much, too. He said":

The water beetle here shall teach
A lesson far beyond your reach.
She aggravates the human race
By gliding on the water's face
Assigning each to each its place.
But if she ever stopped to think
Of how she did it, she would sink.

MORAL: Don't ask questions.

So Elliott and I went fishing.

26 February——————————————

Guess What?

The admiral hated to snoop, so he left the bottle of shampoo just where he had found it—next to the tea and coffee. The bottle had a picture of a llama on the label.

The admiral's wife, who usually wore a gingham dress and moccasins when visiting their ranch on the Nebraska prairie, had just returned from her chores at the bank and the church bazaar. She was now helping the cook make the chowder and the goulash for lunch. The admiral heard them talking in the kitchen.

Someone was playing a ukulele, which the admiral did not like, so he turned on the radio and listened to a pretty mazurka by Chopin. Then he looked through his collection of pictures—mostly of boats, rafts, and kayaks.

When everyone sat down to eat, the principal of the kindergarten cried, "At last! Hurrah!"—and by accident spilled the ketchup all over the taffy apples! This so amused another guest, who had just returned from a safari, that he pulled a toy pistol out of his sack and ran all around the veranda laughing like a maniac and firing his pistol at imaginary zombies.

It was a grand party.

37

Well, reader, do you understand this story? If you do, it means that you understand at least one word from thirty-two different languages! These words, which have become part of English, were born elsewhere.

What are the thirty-two words? Here they are:

the word	comes from	the word	comes from
admiral	Arabic	chowder	Creole
snoop	Dutch	goulash	Hungarian
bottle	Medieval Latin	kitchen	Old Saxon
shampoo	Hindustani	ukulele	Hawaiian
tea	Chinese	mazurka	Polish
coffee	Turkish	rafts	Old Norse
llama	Tibetan	kayaks	Eskimo
gingham	Malay	kindergarten	German
moccasins	Powhatan	hurrah	Slavic
ranch	Spanish	taffy	Tagalog
Nebraska	Sioux	safari	Swahili
prairie	French	pistol	Czech
chores	Greek	sack	Hebrew
bank	Italian	veranda	Portuguese
church	Old Frisian	maniac	Latin
bazaar	Persian	zombies	West African

You should be proud of yourself. I am.

—LEO ROSTEN

27 February

I give a definition, and you turn it into two words that rhyme. I say, for instance, "smelly finger," and you answer, "stinky pinky." Or I say, "unhappy father," and you answer, "sad dad." That is the game that Alexander, Elliott, Medora, and Jeremy (Joanna and Taylor aren't old enough yet to play) call Stinky Pinky. It goes like this:

The Definition	The Stinky Pinky
aviator	fly guy
breakfast fish exporter	kipper shipper
cheerful progenitor	glad dad
chicken purchaser	fryer buyer
dejected cleric	sunk monk

departed spouse	late mate
escaped fowl	loose goose
costly lager	dear beer
funniest joke	best jest
inexperienced monarch	green queen
jumpy fowl	jerky turkey

Take turns with your friends thinking up stinky pinkies.

28 February

Behemoth

"Behold now Behemoth," says God in the Bible. Behemoth sounds very grand, but it is just a good old ugly hippopotamus. I wrote this verse to show that *behemoth* has three different pronunciations, all perfectly acceptable:

BEHOLD NOW Bee-HEE-moth (BEE-hee-MOUTH?
BEE-HEE-MOATH?)

Behold now! By the Jordan dreameth
That beast by scholars called bē-hē′-moth;
Though scholars of another cloth
I understand say bē′-he-mŏth;
While others still, rejecting both,
Refer to him as bē-he-mōth′.
The beast is one, the sound trichotomous;*
The fact is, he's a hip-pō-pŏt′-a-mus.
—W.R.E.

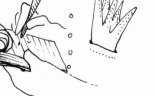

*This means "divided into three parts." See how smart you are getting?

29 February _____

As Saint Patrick Goes Walking

February 29, which comes every fourth year, is the day when, by tradition, a woman can ask a man to marry her instead of the other way around. Here is a story of how the tradition started:

As Saint Patrick goes walking on the banks of Lough Neagg, whom should he meet but Saint Bridget in tears.

"What is it, alanna?"* says he.

"Oh sorrow," says she, "the colleens I'm teaching will be the death of me."

"Why for?"

"They're wantin' the right to be married, and to ask the boys themselves."

"Let them want," says he, "and stop weepin', alanna."

"I can't," says she.

"Then how would it be," says he, "if we let the colleens ask the boys once in seven years?"

"I daren't face them with anything so seldom," says she. Then, taking Patrick's hand in hers, she starts to wheedle. "Let you make it once in four years, darlint!" And Bridget gives his hand a good big squeeze.

"Squeeze me that way again," says Patrick, "and it not only shall be so, but I'll leap another day into the month to give them more of a chance."

Bridget then asks, "And if the boys say no?"

"The colleens may claim a forfeit."

"And is this the month it is?"

"This very month."

"And is this the extra day?"

"The day itself."

"Then Patrick, me darlint, will ye marry me?"

"And what of my vow?" says he, taken aback.

"I can't help that," says Bridget, "and plaze for me forfeit I'll have a new silk gown."

The story says that she got a kiss as well.

—ELEANOR FARJEON

*Alanna, or alannah, means "child" in Anglo-Irish.

March

1 March

A THREE-TOED TREE TOAD'S ODE

A tree toad loved a she toad
    That lived high in a tree.
She was a two-toed tree toad
    But a three-toed toad was he.

The three-toed tree toad tried to win
    The she toad's nuptial nod;
For the three-toed tree toad loved the road
    The two-toed tree toad trod.

Hard as the three-toed tree toad tried,
    He could not reach her limb.
From her tree toad bower, with her V-toe power
    The she toad vetoed him.

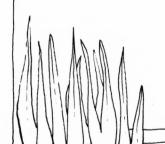

2 March

Kinkering Kongs

If you mean to say "a pretty girl," but reverse letters and say "a gritty pearl" instead, you have made the kind of mistake that is called a *spoonerism*. It is named for William Archibald Spooner, a nineteenth-century clergyman at Oxford University who had a reputation for getting his words twisted.

Dr. Spooner is credited with the spoonerisms below. Decide what he *meant* to say.

1. "Our dear Lord, we know, is a *shoving leopard.*"
2. "We will sing hymn One Seven Five—'*Kinkering Kongs* Their Titles Take.'"
3. "All of us have in our hearts a *half-warmed fish* to lead a better life."

3 March

Betty, my sister, and I fell out.
    And what do you think it was all about?
She loves coffee and I love tea,
    And that is the reason we couldn't agree.

—•—

On Nevski Bridge a Russian stood
Chewing his beard for lack of food.
Said he, "It's tough this stuff to eat
But a darn sight better than shredded wheat."

4 March

It All Deep Ends

Elliott pointed out that a word sometimes can be divided by sound into two or more different words.

"Give me a for instance," I said.

"Purr pull," said Elliott. "Purple."

I began to catch the idea.

"Come, passion," I said. "Compassion. Deep lore. Deplore."

"No bull. Noble."

Alexander said, "Grew some. Gruesome."

"Junk shun. Junction," said Jeremy, getting into the spirit of things. "Judge meant. Judgment. Loan sum. Lonesome. Shall owe. Shallow."

"Sometimes you can divide a word in more than one way," I said. "*Depart* could be either deep art or deep part."

We may play that game again some day. Or we may not.

It all deep ends.

5 March

Let's Eat Daddy

"Let's eat daddy" is a shameful suggestion. But nobody will lift an eyebrow if you say, "Let's eat, daddy." Punctuation makes the difference.

If you say, "The murderer protested his innocence an hour after he was put to death," people will say that is impossible. But they will believe you if you say, "The murderer protested his innocence. An hour after, he was put to death."

There is a great difference between

Mr. Jones, the criminal, has been caught.

and

Mr. Jones, the criminal has been caught.

Or between

Seven people knew the secret, all told.

and

Seven people knew the secret; all told.

Shakespeare played with punctuation in this exchange from *Othello:*

CASSIO: Dost thou hear, my honest friend?

CLOWN: No, I hear not your honest friend; I hear you.

There is a city in Egypt named Said and pronounced Sah-eed. Bearing that in mind, see if you can punctuate this to make sense:

Said I I said you said I said said said he who said I said you said said I said said is said said said is not said said.

6 March——————————————————

Locks and Keys

ALEXANDER: A man who lived alone
lost the keys
to his house
and couldn't get in.
He tried the front door,
but it was locked.
Then he tried
the other doors,
but they were locked.
Then he tried the windows,
but they were locked.
Since he was a poor man,
he did not want
to break a window,
and he could not afford
to have a locksmith come.
But finally he managed
to get in anyway.
How did he do it?

JEREMY: I don't know.

ALEXANDER: After he tried
all the doors
and all the windows,
he began to run
around the house.
He ran around
and around
and around
and around
and around
and around
until at last
he was all in.

("What do you mean, 'all in?'" asked Jeremy. "Totally tired," said
Alexander.)

44

In the land where your left is your right,
You will notice a curious sight:
> At set of the sun
> The day has begun,
And when the sun rises it's night.

———•———

A girl who played baseball at Sears
Reduced her opponents to tears;
> For when batting she swung
> At the ball with her tongue,
And when catching, she caught with her ears.

—W.R.E.

• When a man marries how many wives does he get?
Sixteen: four richer, four poorer, four better, four worse.

• When is an artist unhappy?
When he draws a long face.

• What is it that is always coming but never arrives?
Tomorrow. When it arrives, it is today.

• What has eighteen legs and catches flies?
A baseball team.

• What should a man know before trying to teach a dog?
More than the dog.

• What do you get if you pour boiling water down a rabbit hole?
Hot cross bunnies.

• What do you give a sick pig?
Oinkment.

• What is round and green, is covered with blue hair, has big scaly
  claws, weighs five thousand pounds, and goes peckety-peck-peck?
Nothing.

9 March

ABCD Goldfish

In ABC language, letters of the alphabet and numbers substitute for the words they sound like—I 8 A P, for instance, for "I ate a pea."

AB, or Abie, is a frequent character in these exchanges. He is a grocer below, his part being played by Jeremy:

MEDORA: "AB, F U NE X?"
JEREMY: "S V F X."
MEDORA: "F U NE M?"
JEREMY: "S V F M."
MEDORA: "OK L F M N X."

That is easy to translate—F is have, U is you, NE is any, X is eggs, and so on.

But when Alexander wrote out the ABC passage below, I could not understand it until he explained it to me:

> YY U R
> YY U B
> I C U R
> YY 4 me.

"U R is 'you are,'" I said; "U B is 'you be.' But what do those two Ys mean?"

"You've got it, Pop!" cried Alexander, coming over and shaking my hand: *'too wise' ":*

Too wise you are,
Too wise you be;
I see you are
Too wise for me.

"I knew it all the time," I said.

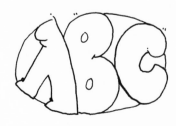

10 March—————————————

Oh Der, Oh Der!

How many *der*'s are there in each line of the verse below? The number will give you the meaning of the verse.

> So der der der der der der der der der the night,
> So der der der der der der der der der the
> voice of the dove
> That a fellow's quite right
> If he der der der der der der der der der der
> his lady his love.
>
> —W.R.E.

11 March—————————————

THE ANSWERS
"When did the world begin and how?"
I asked a lamb, a goat, a cow:

"What's it all about and why?"
I asked a hog as he went by:

"Where will the whole thing end, and when?"
I asked a duck, a goose, a hen:

And I copied all the answers too,
A quack, a honk, an oink, a moo.
> —ROBERT CLAIRMONT

SING SONG

o
da da
o
ma ma
love
me
o
me

o
ma ma
o
da da
love
me

> —ARNOLD ADOFF

12 March

Had I Butt Nude

Butt has several meanings. The butt of a rifle is the thick rear end that the person shooting holds against his (or her) shoulder. The butt of a cigarette is the unburned part. The butt of a joke is someone who is made to look ridiculous. But you have never seen a butt that means what the butt means in the verse below.

A *nude* is someone without clothes. There is a famous picture called *Nude Descending a Staircase,* in which a woman is painted as if she were made of cubes. But that is not what nude means in this verse.

A *dude* is an overdressed man—or, in slang, any man at all. But not here.

A *seed* is what you sow to make crops grow. But not here.

A *deed* is an action—a good deed, a bad deed. But not here.

In fact, those words don't really mean anything in this verse. But somehow they seem to:

Had I butt nude,
  Had I butt seed,
Would I have dude
  The dids I deed?
            —W.R.E.

13 March

Oh, My Aching Stomach

"What was the most unusual meal ever eaten?" asked Elliott.

"I have no idea," I said.

"When Ben Belly came home for dinner, he bolted the door, drank from the bedspring, ate scallops from the curtains and a leak from the faucet, took a few hot dogs he had bread himself, had a roll on the floor, and washed all this down with whine from the cat. Then he took a few dates from the calendar, and a plumb from his carpenter's kit. He also had tea from his golf bag. An hour later he didn't feel so good, and he threw up the window."

I sometimes think Elliott reads the wrong kind of books.

14 March

Who Befriendth?

"Who befriendth?" asked Jeremy. (Jeremy lisps when he is not careful; he has just lost two baby teeth in the top row front, and the teeth that will replace them are not showing yet. But Jeremy is no baby. At seven, he can spell better than some ten-year-olds. He can even move the letters in words around to make other words.)

"You mean 'who befriends,'" said Elliott. "But what does *that* mean? It's silly."

"No it's not," said Jeremy. "*I* befriends, that's who."

"You have to say 'I *befriend*,' not 'I *befriends*,'" said Elliott.

"No, I *befriends*," insisted Jeremy. I'll show you. *Befriends* is spelled b-e-f-r-i-e-n-d-s, isn't it?"

"I guess so," said Elliott.

"All right. Now I'm going to take out the *b*, and juggle the rest of the letters around. Do you know what I get?"

"No, I don't," said Elliott.

"I get d-e-f-i-n-e-r-s. *Definers.* Definers are people who define things. Then I'll drop the *s*, and mix the letters again. And I get r-e-f-i-n-e-d. *Refined.*"

"You are too smart, Jeremy," said Elliott.

"And then I am going to drop one of the *e*'s and juggle the letters again. And I get f-i-n-d-e-r. *Finder.* And then I drop the *f,* and juggle, and get d-i-n-e-r. *Diner.* And then I drop the other *e,* and get r-i-n-d. *Rind.* And then I drop the *r,* and have———"

"D-i-n. *Din,*" said Elliott.

"Yeth—I mean yes. And then I drop the *d,* and have ———"

"In."

"And then I drop the *n,* and what is left?"

"*I,*" said Elliott.

"Yes. *I*. Who befriends? (He said it without lisping this time.) *I* do. I told you so."

"I still don't get it," said Elliott.

Here is how Jeremy shrank *befriends* down to *I:*

BEFRIENDS
DEFINERS
REFINED
FINDER
DINER
RIND
DIN
IN
I

15 March

A Train Load of Names

These names appear in a book by John Train called *Remarkable Names*. He says they are all the names of real people:

- Ave Maria Klinkenberg
- Mrs. Belcher Wack Wack
- Reverend Christian Church
- Hugh Pugh
- John Senior, Junior
- Joy Bank
- Katz Meow
- Miss Pinkey Dickey Dukes
- T. Hee

16 March

Find the Animals

"Why is 'Jeremy is a comical fellow' a special kind of sentence?" asked Alexander.

"Because Jeremy is *not* a comical fellow," said Elliott.

"No," said Alexander, "because the sentence has four letters in a row that spell out the name of an animal." He wrote on a scratchpad:

Jeremy is a comi*CAL F*ellow.

"You see?" he said. "Calf!"

There is an animal hidden in each of the eight sentences below. Can you find them?

1. I am sure most rich people pay taxes.
2. He won't be around much longer.
3. It turned out to be a very pleasant day.
4. The author sent his boy out for more typing paper.
5. Please take the elevator to the fourth floor.
6. Maybe now, or maybe never.
7. I didn't fall; I only thought I might.
8. Where did the commando go after the battle?

17 March

Why Paddy's Not at Work Today

This is Saint Patrick's Day, a good time to read an Irish poem that has been going the rounds since at least the turn of the century. Sometimes it is told about a bricklayer who is *not* Irish; but Paddy in this rhymed version certainly is.

Dear Sir I write this note to you to tell you of me plight
For at the time of writing I am an awful sight
Me body is all black and blue, me face a deathly gray
And I write to you to say why Paddy's not at work today.

While working on the fourteenth floor some bricks I had to clear
To throw them down from such a height was not a good idea
The foreman wasn't very pleased and being a mean old sod
He said I'd have to carry them down the ladder in me hod.

Well to carry down the bricks by hand it was so very slow
So I hoisted up a barrel and secured the rope below
But in me haste to do the job I was too blind to see
That a barrel filled with building bricks was heavier than me.

So when I untied the rope well the barrel fell like lead
And clinging tightly to the rope I started up instead
I shot up like a rocket when to my dismay I found
That halfway up I met the bloody barrel coming down.

Well the barrel broke me shoulder as to the ground it sped
And at the top I hit the bloody pulley with me head
I clung on tight though numb from shock from that almighty blow
The barrel spilled out half the bricks some fourteen floors below.

Yes half the bricks had fallen from the barrel to the floor
I then outweighed the barrel so I started down once more
I clung on tightly to the rope as I sped to the ground
And I landed on the broken bricks a-lying all around.

I lay there a-groaning I thought I'd passed the worst
When the barrel hit the pulley-head and then the bottom burst
A shower of bricks fell down on me 'twas then I gave up hope.
And lying there upon the ground let go the bloody rope.

Well the barrel then was heavier and started down once more
It landed right across me as I lay there on the floor
I broke three ribs and my left arm and I am here to say
I hope you'll understand why Paddy's not at work today.

—SEAN CANNON

(Rob Joel, who sent me this, says it is sung to the tune of "The Garden Where the Praties Grow." Ask your parents if they know it.)

STORY **18 March**————————————————————

My Dad

When Medora is not doing gymnastics,
swimming, playing tennis, riding her
bicycle, or frowning over homework,
she is likely to be drawing pictures
or writing stories. This story is really
a description of her father:

My dad plays the piano so nicly and I dance to the music.

My dad makes speaches all over the World.

He loves to spray cocroches in the midul of the nite when thay come owt of there hiding places.

He gose birding in strange places.

19 March

A Wiggle of Chorus Girls

Jeremy asked why a bunch of foxes is called a *skulk* of foxes, while a bunch of lions is called a *pride* of lions.

"Because lions look proud," I said, "and foxes skulk about. A bunch of school children who have not learned their lesson is an *ignorance* of school children. Don't let me ever catch you in a bunch like that, Jeremy."

As I mentioned last month, words that describe bunches of things are called collective nouns. James Lipton invented these collective nouns to describe people he came across when he attended a musical comedy and went out to supper afterward:

A *wiggle* of chorus girls · A *quaver* of sopranos · A *hack* of smokers · A *click* of photographers · An *indifference* of waiters.

20 March

Profanity of Flowers and Fish

Some perfectly innocent words sound like curses if you say them angrily enough. Take, for instance, the names of certain flowers and shellfish:

Flowers	Shellfish
You devil's bit scabious!	You hairy mopalia!
You dwarf spurge!	You denticulate Donax!
You lousewort!	You speckled Tegula!
You henbit dead nettle!	You wentletrap!
You swine cress!	You measled cowry!
You pignut!	You false cerith!
You moneywort loosestrife!	You dead-man's-fingers!
You creeping toadflax!	You bent-nose macoma!

You might try these out the next time you get mad at your best friend.

- How long will an eight-day clock run without winding?
  It won't run at all.

- Why does a horse have six legs?
  Because he has forelegs in front and two legs behind.

- What did the big toe say to the little toe?
  "Don't look now, but there's a heel following us."

- Take away my first letter; take away my second letter; take away my third letter; all right, take away all my letters, and yet I remain the same. What am I?
  The postman.

- Why is an empty room like a room full of married people?
  Because there isn't a single person in it.

- What is yellow and always points north?
  A magnetized banana.

- What starts with T, ends with T, and is full of T?
  A teapot.

- What squeals more loudly than a pig caught under a fence?
  Two pigs.

- Where was the Declaration of Independence signed?
  At the bottom.

SPRING

Sound the flute!
Now it's mute.
Birds delight
Day and Night;
Nightingale
In the dale,
Lark in Sky,
Merrily,
Merrily, merrily, to welcome in the Year.

Little Boy,
Full of joy;
Little Girl,
Sweet and small;
Cock does crow,
So do you;
Merry voice,
Infant noise,
Merrily, merrily, to welcome in the Year.

Little Lamb
Here I am;
Come and lick
My white neck;
Let me pull
Your soft Wool;
Let me kiss
Your soft face;
Merrily, merrily, we welcome in the Year.

—WILLIAM BLAKE

JOKES **23 March**————————————————————

Ham and Hamlet

Alexander says he read that if a little book is a booklet and a little pig a piglet, then a little bull must be a bullet, a little scar a scarlet, a little toy a toilet, a little wall a wallet, a little pull a pullet, and a little ham a Hamlet. I told him he may be partly right; there is a little ham I know who *thinks* he is a Hamlet.

You Cannot Tell

One day a Chinese farmer found his stable door open, and his only horse gone. Hearing of his loss, his friends came to commiserate. "Oh!" they cried. "What a calamity!" The farmer, who was a philosopher, replied, "You cannot tell. It may prove to be a blessing."

The following day the horse returned, bringing with him a fine mare. Once more the farmer's friends flocked about him. "You have now two horses instead of one," they cried. "What a blessing!" The farmer said, "You cannot tell. It may prove to be a calamity."

The following day the farmer's son rode the new mare; but she was too lively for him; she threw him, and the young man's leg was broken. "Alas!" cried the farmer's friends. "What a calamity!" "You cannot tell," said the farmer; "it may be a blessing."

The following day a war broke out in that part of China; all the young men of the village joined the army, and were killed in battle. All, that is, but the farmer's son, who could not fight because of his broken leg, and lived to farm his father's lands in peace.

Thus you see how many a blessing may give rise to a misfortune, and out of many a misfortune a blessing may spring.

—ELEANOR FARJEON

Töf-töf, Doki-doki

Why is the note of a songbird "tweet-tweet" in your ears, while it is "cui-cui" in the ears of a French boy or girl? My guess, as I said earlier, is that since the bird makes no consonant sound at all, the way the sound was recorded in different languages came about largely by chance. Once we have written down "tweet-tweet," or "cui-cui," that is the way we hear the sound. But there is no way to prove this. After all, one language may have sounds that do not exist in another.

Whatever the reason, your heart beats "pit-a-pat;" Japanese hearts beat "doki-doki." American trains go "toot-toot!" German trains go "töf-töf!"

26 March ─────────────────

LADIES AND JELLYBEANS

Ladies and jellybeans,
Reptiles and crocodiles,
I stand before you
And sit behind you
To tell you something
I know nothing about.
There will be a meeting tomorrow night
Right after breakfast
To decide which color
To whitewash the church.
There is no admission;
Just pay at the door.
There will be plenty of seats,
So sit on the floor.

27 March ─────────────────

Want Ads

Alexander and Elliott claim they found these mistakes in newspaper want ads.

These are Alexander's:

- APARTMENT TO SHARE. Two students at Wellesley College seek well-bred fiend.
- HELP WANTED. Girl to hell with washing and ironing.

These are Elliott's:

- DEPENDABLE FIRM seeks widow-washers. Experience desirable.
- LOST. White spaniel who answers to Lady with black spots on her hindquarters.

Buddy Basch wrote me that he saw a sign in the rear window of a house trailer that was traveling across Florida at sixty miles per hour. The sign said ROOM FOR RENT. Underneath was written in smaller type:
Must be willing to travel.

28 March ————————————————————

JOANNA: Knock, knock.
ALEXANDER: Who's there?
JOANNA: Sarah.
ALEXANDER: Sarah who?
JOANNA: Sarah doctor in the house?

TAYLOR: Knock, knock.
ELLIOTT: Who's there?
TAYLOR: Chester.
ELLIOTT: Chester who?
TAYLOR: Chester minute and I'll try to find out.

JOANNA: Knock, knock.
JEREMY: Who's there?
JOANNA: Minnie.
JEREMY: Minnie who?
JOANNA: Minnie brave hearts lie asleep in the deep.

MEDORA: Knock, knock.
JEREMY: Who's there?
MEDORA: Boo.
JEREMY: Boo hoo?
MEDORA: Don't cry, it's only a joke.

ALEXANDER: Knock, knock.
MEDORA: Who's there?
ALEXANDER: Amos.
MEDORA: Amos who?
ALEXANDER: Amos-quito just bit me.

29 March ———————————————————— LIMERICKS

A gardening nut from O'Hare
Grew apples and grapes in his hair.
One day on the beach
He met a young peach—
Now the peach and the nut are a pear.

Said Bob to his twin brother Pete,
"Since our heads are both made of concrete,
Why don't we use yours
For knocking down doors,
And mine for cementing the street?"

—W.R.E.

WHERE DO
THOSE
WORDS
COME
FROM?

30 March

Kangaroo

Captain James Cook charted the unexplored coast of Australia in 1770. When he went ashore, he saw animals leaping about on large hind legs. Their forelimbs were small, they had a long, tapered tail, and they carried their babies in a stomach pouch. Captain Cook asked what their name was, but the natives did not understand him, and replied with their word for "I don't know"—*kangaroo*. So he called the strange animals kangaroos, and they have been called kangaroos ever since. (Or so the story goes; but I am suspicious. It seems to me they would have said "I don't know" to other questions too, so that most of the animals on the subcontinent would be known today as kangaroos.)

Speaking of Australia, there is an earthworm there that grows to be twelve feet long. Tell your local robin.

CRAZY
GRAMMAR

31 March

A CONSISTENCY OF PLURALS

The plural of tooth is teeth;
Is the plural of booth then beeth?
The plural of mouse is mice;
Is the plural of spouse then spice?
The plural of that is those;
Is the plural of hat then hose,
And the plural of rat then rose?

Who knows?

April

1 April

APRIL

APRIL's named for APHRODITE,
Who goes to bed without a nightie.
— W.R.E.

HAPPY BIRTHDAY, JEREMY!

On April first young Jeremy was born, and (I suppose)
At once said to his mother, "There's a spider on
    your nose!"
When mama screamed he laughed and laughed till he
    began to drool,
And said, "Don't call me Jeremy, just call me April
    Fool!"
— W.R.E.

APRIL

April, April,
Laugh thy girlish laughter;
Then, the moment after,
Weep thy girlish tears!
April, that mine ears
Like a lover greetest,
If I tell thee, sweetest,
All my hopes and fears,
April, April,
Laugh thy golden laughter;
But, the moment after,
Weep thy golden tears!
— WILLIAM WATSON

2 April

GH EAU GHT EIGH PT OUGH

Pronounce GH like P, as in hiccough.
Pronounce EAU like O, as in plateau.
Pronounce GHT like T, as in naught.
Pronounce EIGH like A, as in neigh.
Pronounce PT like T, as in pterodactyl.
Pronounce OUGH like O, as in though.
What do you have? Well, the word you have spelled out is
gh eau ght eigh pt ough, *gheaughteighptough.*
But the word you have pronounced is *potato.*

3 April

THERE WAS AN OLD WOMAN

There was an old woman who swallowed a fly;
I wonder why
She swallowed a fly.
Poor old woman, she's sure to die.

There was an old woman who swallowed a spider,
That went oops-oops right down inside her;
She swallowed the spider to catch the fly,
I wonder why
She swallowed a fly.
Poor old woman, she's sure to die.

There was an old woman who swallowed a bird;
How absurd
To swallow a bird.
She swallowed the bird to catch the spider (etc.)

There was an old woman who swallowed a cat;
Fancy that!
She swallowed a cat (etc.)

There was an old woman who swallowed a dog;
She went the whole hog
And swallowed a dog (etc.)

There was an old woman who swallowed a cow;
I wonder how
She swallowed a cow (etc.)

There was an old woman who swallowed a horse . . .
She died, of course!

4 April —————————————————————— REBUSES

Stool/He Fell/Stool

Every time Alexander mows the lawn, his father pays him a dollar. Alexander says he is going on strike because a dollar is not enough. He has written out a picket sign, and says he will march back and forth with it in front of his house. The sign reads:

I have to   paid
_____ because _____
    work   I am

I said, "But the sign doesn't mean anything."
"Oh yes it does, Pop," said Alexander. And he showed me:

I have to
_____ stands for "I have to *over*work."
work

     paid
And   _____ stands for "I am *under*paid."
     I am

Put it all together, and the sign says, "I have to overwork because I am underpaid."

Alexander's picket sign was a rebus, which, as I told you before, is a riddle where symbols or pictures stand for words. Here are two more rebuses:

stool/He fell/stool

and

5 April————————————————————

If two's company and three's a crowd
    And bees live in a hive,
Tell me now, for crying out loud,
    What are four and five?
Nine.

Has eighty-eight keys
    And needs no more,
But can't unlock
    A single door.
A piano.

Round as a wheel,
    Hollow as a cup,
Forty thousand elephants
    Couldn't pull it up.
A well.

Why do you suppose
    It would be all wrong
If your pretty nose
    Were twelve inches long?
Then it would be a foot.

'Tis true I have both face and hands,
    And move before your eyes;
Yet when I go my body stands,
    And when I stand I lie.
A clock.

—ENNIS REES

6 April————————————————————

"Think of a number," said Elliott. Alexander thought of a number.
"Double it." Alexander doubled it.
"Add four." He added four.
"Divide by two." He divided by two.
"Add seven." He added seven.
"Multiply by eight." He multiplied by eight.
"Subtract twelve." He subtracted twelve.
"Divide by four." He divided by four.
"Subtract fifteen." He subtracted fifteen.
"Divide by two." He divided by two.
"You are now back to the number you first thought of," said Elliott.
And he was.

7 April

PROPPER ENGLISH

Once upon a time I used
To mispell
To sometimes split infinitives
To get words of out order
To punctuate, badly
To confused my tenses
to ignore capitals
To employ "common or garden" clichés
To exaggerate hundreds of times a day
But worst of all I used
To forget to finish what I
　　　　—ALAN F. G. LEWIS

8 April

Hobson-Jobsons

A long time ago, British colonists in India heard crowds of Moslems—followers of the prophet Muhammad—wailing, "O Hasan! O Hosain!" The Moslems were mourning the deaths more than a thousand years ago of two grandsons of the prophet. Because Hasan and Hosain were strange words to the British, they substituted the good old English names Hobson and Jobson. Any change of a foreign word into a common English word of much the same sound is now called a hobson-jobson. Here are a few:

- Your little finger is called a pinky, but not because it is pink. The word comes from the Dutch *pinkje,* meaning "small."
- You say, "I don't give a hoot," but the hoot has nothing to do with hooting. It means "a very small amount," and is a corruption of *iota,* the name of the ninth and smallest Greek letter ("I" in English).
- You say, "The room is in apple pie order," but not in reference to apple pie. You are mispronouncing *nappe plié,* French for "neatly folded linen."
- You may call a stupid person a nitwit, but the word does not refer to his wits; it comes from the Dutch *niet wiet,* "I don't know."
- To curry favor is to try to gain favor by fawning and flattery. In a fourteenth-century French satire, anyone wanting a favor from the king would offer to curry his yellow horse, named Favel. The expression first came into English as "curry Favel," and was soon hobson-jobsoned into "curry favor."

9 April

A Square Meal

WHAT DID THE WORLD'S CHAMPION EATER DO TO WIN HIS TITLE?

Across

1 Masculine pronoun
3 _____ up (exploded)
7 Where tolls (charges for driving over a bridge or a road) are collected
10 "_____ pocket full of rye"
11 Everyone; everything
12 Like a heated oven
14 Track _____ field
16 "I've been to London to look _____ the queen"
17 Boy's name
18 In school, be promoted two grades at one time
20 Pretty, popular girl; _____ of the ball
22 Red Cross (abbreviation)
24 Marquis _____ Lafayette, French hero of the American Revolution
25 Tale
28 Entrance to a building or a room
32 Belonging to the girl
33 Short for "Electrical Engineer"
34 Lamb's mother
35 "There was an old woman who lived _____ shoe"
36 Large deer
38 Letter for "East" on a compass
39 Gulped
43 Tall shade trees
44 20 (Roman numeral)

Down

1 "Yo-ho-_____"
2 Railway above a street
3 Fastened with a bolt; swallowed hastily
4 _____ and behold!
5 Girl's name
6 _____-wheat bread
7 Gas or gasoline is kept in a _____
8 Sixth note of the musical scale
9 Give away a secret
13 Seventh note of the musical scale
14 Wise _____ an owl
15 501 (Roman numeral)
19 In favor of; for
21 Was in first place
23 Fishermen's wicker baskets (rhymes with "eels")
25 Become aware of; feel
26 Net dragged by a fishing boat along the sea bottom
27 Scream
29 Short for "Old English"
30 Was indebted to
31 Prefix meaning "again"
32 Nickname for "Hiram"
37 In boxing, a knockout
40 You are; I _____
41 Letters between UV and YZ
42 _____-president (former president)

(Answer to question in title:)

___ ___ ___ ___ ___ ___
1 Across 3 Down

___ ___ ___ ___ ___ ___
10 Across 28 Across

___ ___ ___ ___
14 Across

___ ___ ___ ___ - ___ ___ ___ ___ ___
39 Across

___ ___ ___ ___ ___ ___ ___ ___ ___ ___ ___ ___ ___ !
10 Across 6 Down 25 Across

—RUTH LAKE TEPPER

10 April

As I Lay Dying

Arthur Roth suggests that the last words of a dying elevator operator might well be, "Going up?" And he suggests these last words for other kinds of specialists:

- An atheist: "I was kidding all along."
- A student: "I fail."
- A lawyer: "My final brief."
- An undertaker: "I'm off on a busman's holiday."
- A childless railroad conductor: "End of the line."
- A bridge player: "I pass."
- A gossip: "I'm just dying to tell someone."

11 April ————————————————————————

A lady in London, when found
In a spherical home underground,
    Explained, "I'm too fat
    To live in a flat,
But I do very well in a round."

————•————

A hawk fell in love with an auk
Who never had learned how to talk.
    "Dear, give me a sign
    Just to prove that you're mine,"
Begged the hawk; and the awk replied, "Squawk!"

—W.R.E.

12 April ————————————————————————

The Carping Critics

The suffix *-est* means "most," so it is wrong to use most and *-est* together; but Shakespeare said "the most unkindest cuts," so I don't see why I shouldn't. Besides, I like the sound. These are "unkindest cuts" by critics about plays and actors.

- Robert Benchley, reviewing a comedy that was not very comic: "Some laughter was heard in the back row. Someone must have been telling jokes back there."
- A critic called Mr. Blank the worst actor living. Next play around, he wrote: "Mr. Blank's performance was not up to its usual standard."
- Monty Woolley's report on a dull show: "For the first time in my life I envied my feet. They were asleep."
- "The actor who took the role of King Lear last night played the king as though he expected someone to play the ace."
- A play called *A Good Time* opened in London. The complete review: "No."
- "Last night the high school band played Mozart. Mozart lost."
- Alexander Woolcott: "The scenery was beautiful—but the actors got in front of it."

YOU BRING OUT THE BEAST IN ME

Am I a man? Am I a mouse? Well, you
Might say I'm all the creatures in the zoo.
I'm peacock-proud. I'm gentle as a lamb.
I'm stubborn as a mule. I also am
As strong as oxen; mangy as a dog.
I have the table manners of a hog.
My appetite is birdlike.* When I woo,
My eyes are calf-eyes; like a dove's my coo.
I am goose-silly; fleeter than a deer.
I'm nervous as a cat, and what I hear
I parrot. I am wiser than an owl.
I strut as grandly as a rooster; howl
As wolves do, or coyotes. Too, I screech
Like any peacock; hang on like a leech.
I'm slippery as eels, and hungrier
Than bears; yet kitten-like's my purr;
My chatter, like a magpie's. Worse than that,
I have been called a worm—a louse—a rat.
I'm pigeon-toed, and busy as a bee—
A Bengal tiger in ferocity.
I'm busy as a beaver, turtle-slow,
And chicken-livered. You should also know
My neighbors say I drink much like a fish. . . .
(Please add as many creatures as you wish.)
—W.R.E.

*Why do we say a small appetite is birdlike? Birds eat all day long.

14 April————————————————————

Happy Birthday, Medora!

The middle name of Medora's mother is Medora. The first name of her great-aunt was Medora. The middle name of her great-grandmother was Medora. The middle name of her great-great-grandmother was Medora. And the middle name of her great-great-great-grandmother was Medora.

So, today being Medora's birthday, I wrote her this poem about her name:

> Medora bore a-
> nother Medora
> (This story, Medora,
>   Is true)—
> Who bore encore a-
> *nother* Medora,
> Who opted for a-
> *nother* Medora,
> Who raised the score a-
> *nother* Medora.
> Now who's once more a-
> NOTHER Medora?
> It's *you*, Medora,
>   It's *you*!

Medora is now eight years old. She received this birthday card, and here is what the birthday card said:

> What brings 8 funny riddles
> for someone nice who's 8
>   And wishes for a day
>   that's fun to celebrate?
>
> (In case you need a clue—
> it's this birthday card for you!)

Can you answer these riddles about 8?

1. Why did the baker stop making doughnuts after 8 years?
2. Where does 8 come before 7?
3. When do 8 and 8 make more than 16?
4. What 8-letter word has all the letters in it?

5. What has 8 legs and sings?
6. If you ask any 8 people to pronounce a certain word, all 8 will pronounce it wrong. What is the word?
7. Where was Henry VIII crowned?
8. How much dirt is there in a hole 8 feet long, 8 feet wide, and 8 feet deep?

15 April

Foreign Dogs Can't Bark English

If you study a foreign language and have no reason to use it you may think you have forgotten it. But it is still hiding someplace inside of you.

Alexander learned to speak Spanish before he spoke English. But when he was two years old, his father was transferred from Bolivia to Uganda. From then on Alexander refused to speak Spanish any longer. He would speak only English and Swahili, which is the language of the Ugandans.

But one day, when Alexander was four, he rediscovered a picture book with Spanish captions that he had loved in Bolivia. He turned the pages, and as he saw the pictures—a ball, an apple, a banana—he quite unconsciously named them aloud, one after another, in Spanish, as he had nearly three years before.

I suspect that even now, when he is twelve years old, Alexander does not hear animal sounds in quite the way we do; he also hears them the way they sound to someone who speaks Spanish, or Swahili, or Portuguese. (He has lived in Brazil too.) People who speak still other languages hear animals in still different ways.

The barking of a dog sounds to Americans like "bow-wow," "woof-woof," "yap-yap," or "arf-arf." But a dog barks "guau-guau" or "pan-pan" in Spain, "wang-wang" or "wah-wah" in China, "ham-ham" in Rumania, "ouah-ouah" in France, "haf-haf" in Germany, "ha-ha" or "hov-hov" in Turkey, and "bu-bu" in Italy.

Our pigs grunt "oink-oink." In France they grunt "oui-oui" ("oui-oui" means "yes-yes" in French); in Russia, "khru-khru," and in Rumania "guits-guits."

16 April————————————————————

The Cleverest Son

Mala Powers has stories of all kinds for those who dial her "Children's Story" telephone number.* This is a "once upon a time" story:

A rich old man became very ill and called his three sons to him. "I shall reward the son who is the cleverest," he said. "Each of you take one dollar and buy something that will fill my room."

The oldest son quickly went to the market and bought straw. The second son thought a moment, then bought feathers. The youngest son thought and thought, "What can I buy for a dollar that will fill a whole room?" At last he found his answer and made a purchase.

That evening, the three sons returned to their father's room, each with his gift. The oldest son spread his straw, but it covered only one small corner; the second son scattered his feathers, but they filled only two corners.

Quietly, the youngest son took out a candle and lit it with a match. The whole dark room filled with a warm glow.

The old father happily smiled and said, "Though you are my youngest, you are the cleverest and I give to you my lands and money, knowing you will manage them wisely for the family."

*In New York City it's 976-3636; when dialing outside the area, dial 1-212-976-3636.

17 April————————————————————

A moron is a person who is far from being smart. For years people have been making up stories about a boy called the Little Moron.

MEDORA: Why do you have that rope hanging from a tree outside your window, little moron?
JEREMY: To tell the weather. When the rope wiggles, it's windy. When it's wet, it's rainy.

ELLIOTT: Why did the little moron lock his father in the refrigerator?
ALEXANDER: Because he wanted cold pop.

JEREMY: Why did the little moron take hay to bed with him?
ELLIOTT: To feed his nightmare.

The little moron was nailing boards on the side of a house. Another little moron asked him why he was throwing half of the nails away.

"Because the heads are on the wrong ends."

"You numbskull! Those are for the other side of the house."

The little moron was on his hands and knees on Main Street.

"Lose something?" asked a policeman.

"Yes—I dropped a dollar bill on Maple Street."

"Then why are you looking for it on Main Street?"

"Because the light's better here," said the little moron.

18 April ——————————————————— NUMBERS FUN

There were 710
Women and men
At sea in a boat
That ceased to float.

When it spun around
And turned upside down,
What was left then
Of the 710?

(Turn 710 upside down to get the answer.)

—ENNIS REES

Numbers do not always tell the truth. Take, for instance, this one:

317

Turn it upside down, and you have

LIE

The numbers for some years read the same upside down as rightside up. Two of these are 1881 and 1961.

—F. EMERSON ANDREWS

Elliott's teacher told him he could play tricks with the number 9. Here is one of the tricks:

$0 \times 9 + 1 = 1$

$1 \times 9 + 2 = 11$

$12 \times 9 + 3 = 111$

$123 \times 9 + 4 = 1111$

$1234 \times 9 + 5 = 11111$

$12345 \times 9 + 6 = 111111$

$123456 \times 9 + 7 = 1111111$

$1234567 \times 9 + 8 = 11111111$

$12345678 \times 9 + 9 = 111111111$

$123456789 \times 9 + 10 = 1111111111$

19 April

Ay, Aw Ae Oo

"What is the difference between a consonant and a vowel, Pop?" asked Medora.

I rubbed my chin.

"Don't you *know*, Pop?" asked Jeremy.

"Of *course* I know," I said. "It is just a little hard to explain. To talk, you push an air stream out of your mouth. When you stop the flow of air with your tongue or your lips, the break makes a sound called a consonant. The kind of consonant depends on the way you block off the sound. Try making a *b, c, d, f,* and the other consonants. Your tongue and lips are in a different position for each one."

"What about vowels?" asked Elliott.

"That's the sound of the air flow before it's blocked off."

I was not sure my explanation was satisfactory, but it was the best I could do, so I hurried on:

"People who live in the Lowlands of Scotland sometimes leave consonants out of words altogether. A conversation between a Scottish farmer and a storekeeper goes this way:

"The farmer takes a fabric from the counter, and asks, 'Oo?'

" 'Ay, oo.'

" 'Aw oo?'

" 'Ay, aw oo.'

" 'Aw ae oo?'

" 'Ay, aw ae oo.' "

Medora said, "That doesn't make sense."

"It does too. The farmer said, 'Wool?' The storekeeper answered, 'Ay, wool.' The farmer said, 'All wool?' The storekeeper said, 'Aye, all wool.' The farmer said, 'All white wool?' And the storekeeper said, 'Ay, all white wool.' "

What Does # Mean?

There is no one definition of the symbol #. It has at least nine distinct meanings. See how many you can identify in the verse below.

> Many names have I to cumber*
> Me upon my rounds:
> 1. Before a digit, I'm a #;
> 2. After digits, #;
> 3. In a printer's proof, a #;
> While, if at the harp
> You should pluck me from my place,
> 4. I would be a #.
> 5. In one game, I'm #;
> 6. An # on phones.
> 7. In business, I'm #, although
> 8. A # when in bones.
> And in computer language, sir,
> 9. They call me a #.
>
> —W.R.E.

*To load down, that is.

Something Went Wrong

An elderly London lady called on a rescue team to save her cat, which had climbed into a tree and could not make its way down. When they retrieved it the old lady was so grateful that she invited them in for tea. Departing with her thanks ringing in their ears, they failed to notice the cat in the road, ran over it, and killed it.

———•———

A bank robber in Portland, Oregon, held up a paper for the teller to read. Written on it was "This is a holdup and I've got a gun." He then wrote, "Put all the money in a paper bag," and pushed the message across the counter. The teller wrote on the bottom, "I don't have a paper bag," and passed the paper back. The robber fled.

22 April

Mosey, Alabaster

In the nineteenth century Jewish peddlers made the rounds of isolated American farms offering combs, hairpins, ribbons, fabrics, brooches, and other pretties to housewives. Moses being a common Jewish name, when one of the peddlers appeared, the children would rush into the house shouting, "Mama, Moses is coming!" The *s* at the end of the name sloughed off, and the peddlers were called Mosey. Their shuffling, sidling gait, caused by the burden of the packs on their shoulders, was soon called by the same name, and some people believe that is why a shuffling gait is known as *moseying* to this day.

—•—

Fifteen hundred years before Christ, Egyptians worshipped the cat-headed goddess Bast, patroness of lovers and cats. Cats were themselves objects of worship in Egypt. When one died, its owner would mummify the body, lay it out in a coffin carved from a smooth, hard mineral found in the neighborhood, and store it away in a crypt of her temple at the town of Bubastis ("the house of Bast"). The mineral, in honor of the goddess and the town, came to be called *a la Bast*. Today, four thousand five hundred years later, the mineral from which those cat-coffins were made is still called *alabaster*, after the goddess and her town.

23 April

They Have Irish Bulls

An Irish bull is a statement that makes no sense and often contradicts itself. Carl Sandburg put Irish bulls into a poem:

> They have Irish bulls timeworn and mossgrown:
> You are to be hanged and I hope it will prove a
>   warning to you.
> I took so much medicine I was sick a long time after
>   I got well.
> I can never get these boots on until I have worn
>   them for awhile.
> One of us must kill the other—let it be me. We
>   were boys together—at least I was.
> If all the world were blind what a melancholy sight
>   it would be.

This will last forever and afterward be sold for
    old iron.
They would cut us into mincemeat and throw our
    bleeding heads on the table to stare us in the face.
On the dim and far-off shores of the future we can see
    the footprints of the unseen hand.
We pursue the shadow, the bubble bursts, and leaves
    in our hand only ashes.
      —CARL SANDBURG

24 April — THE SEASONS

THE RETURN OF SPRING

Now Time throws off his cloak again
Of ermined frost, and wind, and rain,
And clothes him in the embroidery
Of glittering sun and clear blue sky.
With beast and bird the forest rings,
Each in his jargon cries or sings;
And Time throws off his cloak again
Of ermined frost, and wind, and rain.

River, and fount, and tinkling brook
Wear in their dainty livery
Drops of silver jewelry;
In new-made suit they merry look;
And Time throws off his cloak again
Of ermined frost, and wind, and rain.
      —CHARLES D'ORLEANS
      (translated by
Henry Wadsworth Longfellow)

25 April — LIMERICKS

There was a red hen from Saint Meg
Who laid a remarkable egg.
    At a snap of my thumb
    It would play dead or come;
Roll over, or sit up and beg.
      —W.R.E.

A High that was learning to Low
Met a Stop that was learning to Go.
They walked hand in hand
Till they came to the land
Of a Yes that was learning to No.
—W.R.E.

When a bat ate a spider in Glynn,
The spider proceeded to spin
A web where he traps
All the bugs the bat snaps.
The bat has grown shockingly thin.
—W.R.E.

CRAZY GRAMMAR   **26 April**————————————————

Words that Change Their Minds

What does "to think better of" mean?

1. To like or admire something more than previously: "I *think better of* your judgment than I once did."

2. To like or admire something less than previously: "I was planning to buy the clock, but I *thought better of* it and didn't buy it."

What does "to best" mean?
To defeat: "The Yankees *bested* the Orioles in the eighth inning."

What does "to worst" mean?
The same thing:
"The Yankees *worsted* the Orioles in the eighth inning."

What does "mean" mean?

It means to describe: "A wren *means* a certain kind of bird." It means to intend: "I *mean* to fly that kite." It means lacking in kindness and good-will: "I *mean* you're a *mean* girl." It means occupying a middle position: "I *mean* you should hew to the golden *mean*."

So when you use a word like *mean,* be sure you know what you mean.

78

> Poor Martha Snell
> Her's gone away
> Her would if her could
> But her couldn't stay;
> Her had two swoln legs
> And a baddish cough
> But her legs it was
> As carried her off

From a hypochondriac's tombstone:

I TOLD YOU I WAS SICK

Business and sentiment are mixed here:

> Sacred to the remains of
> Jonathan Thompson
> A pious Christian and
> Affectionate husband
>
> His disconsolate widow
> Continues to carry on
> His grocery business
> At the old stand on
> Main Street; cheapest
> And best prices in town

> Don't worry if your job is small,
> And your rewards are few.
> Remember that the mighty oak
> Was once a nut like you.

———•———

> 'Tis dog's delight to bark and bite
> And little birds to sing,
> And if you sit on a red-hot brick
> It's a sign of an early spring.

Olakgoonb

Can you make a long book from OLAKGOONB? You can: juggle the letters, and you will get A LONG BOOK.

OLAKGOONB is not a real word, but often the letters making up real words can be arranged to make other real words. These rearrangements are called *anagrams.* For example, *but* can be made into *tub, rate* into *tear,* and *how* into *who* (or the other way around).

In this couplet, the two missing words are anagrams of each other:

The schoolbell __ __ __ __, and class begins.
The pupils weep; the teacher __ __ __ __ __.

The answer is easy, because you know what a schoolbell does—it *rings.* And you know that the second missing word has to end in *i n s,* because it rhymes with *begins.* So—*grins.*

Find the missing anagrams in the two verses below:

The bat flies in, the bat flies out;
He __ __ __ __ __ his wings, and __ __ __ __ __ about.

(One of the missing words means "raises, elevates." The other means "flutters, darts.")

"__ __ __ __!" go the scissors;
"__ __ __ __!" goes the top.
Jane __ __ __ __ her skirt on;
The dog __ __ __ __ the cop.

(Think of what a top does, or of the sound scissors make.)

Great virtues have I,
There's none can deny,
And to this I shall mention an odd one:
When applied to the tail
'Tis seldom I fail
To make a good boy of a bad one.

————•————

With words unnumber'd I abound;
In me mankind do take delight;
In me much learning's to be found;
Yet I can neither read nor write.

May

1 May

MAY

MAY comes from MAIA. Very well:
But who was MAIA? Few can tell.*
                                              —W.R.E.

If you tease your cat on May day, it may turn into a witch.

The plural of rhinoceros is rhinoceroses. Still, as this unknown author makes clear, it is easy to get mixed up:

RHINOCEROSES

No one for spelling at a loss is
Who boldly spells Rhinoceroses;
I've known a few (I can't say lots)
Who call the beasts Rhinocerots,
Though they are not so bad, say I,
As they who say Rhinoceri.
One I have heard (O holy Moses!)
Who plainly said Rhinoceroses,
Another one—a brilliant boy—
Insists that it's Rhinoceroi—
The moral that I draw from these is
The plural's what one darn well pleases.

*But I can. To the ancient Greeks Maia was the mother of Hermes, the messenger-God. To the Romans she was goddess of growth. The name means mother or nurse. And I have two friends named Maia. One is Maia Fong and one is Maia Skolnik.

Rhinoceroses seem to me to be a very good subject for May Day, because they have absolutely nothing to do with it:

> *RHINOCEROS STEW*
> If you want to make a rhinoceros stew
> all in the world that you have to do
> is skin a rhinoceros, cut it in two
> and stew it and stew it and stew it.
>
> When it's stewed so long that you've quite forgot
> what it is that's bubbling in the pot
> dish it up promptly, serve it hot
> and chew it and chew it and chew it
> and chew it and chew it and chew it
> and chew it and chew it and chew it.

AND CHEW IT AND CHEW IT AND CHEW IT

—MILDRED LUTON

2 May

Shrinking Drafting into A

Elliott shrank *drafting* down to *a* by dropping one letter at a time, using the remaining letters each time to make a new word. This is how he did it:

- First he dropped the *f* from *drafting,* and shuffled the remaining letters to make

  t-r-a-d-i-n-g
- Then he dropped the *d* from *trading,* and shuffled the letters to make
  r-a-t-i-n-g
- Then he dropped the *g* from *rating,* and shuffled the letters to make
  t-r-a-i-n
- Then he dropped the *i* from *train,* and shuffled the letters to make
  r-a-n-t
- Then he dropped the *r* from *rant,* and had
  a-n-t

- Then he dropped the *t* from *ant,* and had
  a-n
- Then he dropped the *n* from *an,* and had
  a

DRAFTING

TRADING

RATING

TRAIN

RANT

ANT

AN

A

ON-O-MAT-
O-POE-IA

3 May

Streams Babble Chains Clink

What is the name for words like *buzz, cuckoo,* and *hiss,* which sound like what they mean? It is *onomatopoeia,* pronounced *on-o-mat-o-pee-a,* which comes from two Greek words meaning "to coin names." This poem points out that the sounds made by cats and cows do not sound the same to the English as they do to Americans:

PHILOLOGICAL

The British puss demurely mews;
His transatlantic kin meow.
The kine* in Minnesota moo;
Not so the gentle Devon cows:
    They low,
As every schoolchild ought to know.
—JOHN UPDIKE

The onomatopoeic sounds here are strung together with rhyme, but without reason:

VILLAGE AFTERNOON
Streams babble chains clink
Katydid bobolink
Whippoorwill chickadee

*Kine was once the usual plural of *cow.* But most people just say *cows* nowadays.

Endlessly
Call katydid bobolink
Whippoorwill chickadee
Crack whip yap dog
Clop Doggin jog-jog
Whinny mare bleat goat
Baa sheep oink stoat
Horn a-hoot snake a-hiss
Frog a-croak girl a-kiss
Beat hearts creak bones
Clishmaclaver cluck crones
Kodaks clicking dentures clacking
Birds a-twitter ducks quacking
Listen how the skylark savors
Hemidemisemiquavers.

—W.R.E.

4 May

Jeans, Denims, Dungarees

Alexander wears jeans, Elliott wears denims, Medora wears dungarees. Jeremy wears jeans, Joanna wears denims, Taylor wears dungarees. They all look alike.

Jeans, denims, and dungarees are trousers made of sturdy cotton fabric, suitable for rough wear. Nowadays, though, they have become fashionable, and are styled by famous designers, and cost—I won't say an arm and a leg, since after all they *are* trousers; no, they cost two legs.

What is the difference between jeans, denims, and dungarees? As far as the original fabric is concerned, not much. But the names are different because the same sort of cloth was developed in three different places. *Denim* comes *"de* (from) *Nîmes,"* a manufacturing city once prominent in central France. The cloth for *jeans* was woven in Genoa, which the French used to call *Gênes*, and *dungarees* were made in *Dhungaree,* India.

A famous brand of jeans—or denims, or dungarees—is named *Levi's* after Levi Strauss, who developed them. Levi Strauss was a peddler who crossed the Great Plains during the gold rush of the late 1840s. In San Francisco he made work pants for the miners, strengthening the pockets with copper rivets, so that they would not tear when loaded with tools or samples of gold ore. Though the gold rush days have been over for nearly a century and a half, Levi's are still made with those copper rivets.

5 May ———————————————————————

THE FROG

What a wonderful bird the frog are!
When he stand, he sit almost;
When he hop, he fly almost.
He ain't got no sense hardly.
He ain't got no tail hardly either.
When he sit, he sit on what he ain't got almost.

THAT LIFE'S UNFAIR

That life's unfair's a fact well-knowed
   That children must grow useter;
As the crow knowed well, when the rooster crowed,
   That the crow could never rooster.

           —W.R.E.

6 May ———————————————————————

Which goes through the plank first, the bullet
   or the hole?

Where does the music go when the fiddle is put in
   the box?

Where does your lap go when you stand up? The
   same place your fist goes when you open your hand.

What are the two smallest things mentioned in the
   Bible? The widow's mite and the wicked flea.

Who are the shortest people mentioned in the Bible?
   Bildad the Shuhite, Knee-high-miah, and the man
   who had nothing but from whom even that which he
   had was taken away.

What was the last thing Paul Revere said to his
   horse on the famous ride? "Whoa!"

"Did you hear about the empty barrel of flour?"
   "No." "Nothing in it."

What is there more of in the world than anything
   else? Ends.

          —CARL SANDBURG

7 May ——————————————————

How Do I Love Thee?

Elizabeth Barrett Browning wrote a famous love sonnet that begins, "How do I love thee? Let me count the ways." Here is how people with different jobs might count the ways:

- The cardiologist: With all my heart
- The marathon runner: All the way
- The Indian: Without reservation
- The contortionist: Head over heels
- The psychoanalyst: Unshrinkingly
- The elephant trainer: Roguishly
- The mink farmer: Furtively
- The farmer: Whole hog

8 May ——————————————————

Seventeen Elephants

This story comes from India.

A rich man died and left seventeen elephants to his three sons. His will said, "My eldest son gets half of my elephants, my middle son gets one-third, and my youngest son one-ninth of the seventeen elephants."

But there is no way you can divide seventeen elephants that way, unless you cut up one of the elephants. Fortunately, though, a wise old friend had an idea. He lined up their seventeen elephants. Then he added one of his own—so they had *eighteen* elephants. Listen carefully!

Now it was easy—the eldest son got his half—nine elephants—the middle son got one-third of the eighteen, or six elephants—and the youngest son got one-ninth—two elephants. Add them up, you get seventeen. There was one elephant left.

The sons thanked the wise old man who said, "Now I can have my own elephant back." And everyone was happy.

—MALA POWERS

9 May————————————————————————————

A Hundred Words Once

Could you write a composition of one hundred words without repeating a single word? I expect it would take you a long time. But it would not take so long with help from your friends. At a school in Pompton Lakes, New Jersey, Pearl L. Feldman's class put together this example (fudging just a bit by using proper names):

> Let's go! The challenge is to write a composition without using any word more than once. Do you think that it can be done? If not, give one reason for doing this. While we are sitting here in English class at Pompton Lakes School, on Lakeside Avenue, New Jersey, all of us figure out something which makes sense. Mrs. Feldman helps her pupils because another teacher said they couldn't accomplish such tasks. Nobody has fresh ideas right now. Goal—100! How far did students get? Eighty-five finished already; fifteen left. "Pretty soon none!" says Dennis O'Neill. Gary Putnam and Debra Petsu agree. So there!

10 May————————————————————————————

SAY, DID YOU SAY?

Say, did you say, or did you not say
  What I said you said?
  For it is said that you said
  That you did not say
  What I said you said.
  Now if you say that you did not say
  What I said you said,
  Then what do you say you did say instead
  Of what I said you said?

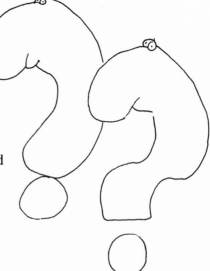

11 May

Little Audrey is the girl who just laughed and laughed as disaster struck her family, her friends, and herself. She was regularly killed, only to appear as lively as ever in another Little Audrey story:

Once upon a time Little Audrey got lost on a desert island. Along came a big bunch of black cannibals and kidnapped her. They tied her up to a tree and started their pot to boiling. Little Audrey knew they were going to make stew of her; so she looked around at those lean, hungry cannibals and counted them. There were nineteen. Little Audrey just laughed and laughed 'cause she knew she was not big enough to make enough stew to go around.

·

Little Audrey and her mama and papa and her little brunette sister were sitting at the dinner table. Papa said, "Little Audrey, pass the cream, please." So Little Audrey passed the cream to her papa, and he poured some into his coffee. Then he put the pitcher down, and Little Audrey noticed that right on the tip end of the spout there was a little drop of cream all ready to fall. Little Audrey just laughed and laughed, 'cause she knew all the time that the little cream pitcher couldn't go *sniff, sniff.*

12 May

A girl who had ears so gigantic
She used them to fly the Atlantic
    Hit windstorms terrific
    Above the Pacific.
End of girl, end of ears, end of antic.
        —W.R.E.

A watch and a clock bet a crown
Over which was the fastest in town.
    To show off their skill
    They ran up a hill;
But half the way up they ran down.
        —W.R.E.

13 May

In a usual palindrome, it is the *letters* of the word or phrase or sentence that read the same forward or backward. (Remember "Madam, I'm Adam"?) In a word palindrome, it is the *words* that can be read either way. Here are four word palindromes:

- "He is so patient a doctor, to doctor a patient so!" "Is he?"
- You can cage a swallow, can't you, but you can't swallow a cage, can you?
- Bores are people that say that people are bores.
- Women understand men; few men understand women.

14 May

A Pretty Deer

Do you know the name for a word that sounds like another, and perhaps is spelled the same, but has an entirely different meaning? It is *homonym.* Find the homonyms in this poem:

> A pretty deer is dear to me,
> A hare with downy hair;
> A hart I love with all my heart,
> But barely bear a bear.

> 'Tis plain that no one takes a plane
> To get a pair of pears,
> Although a rake may take a rake
> To tear away the tares.

> Beer often brings a bier to man,
> Coughing a coffin brings,
> And too much ale will make us ail,
> As well as other things.

Quails do not quail before a storm,
　　A bough will bow before it;
No human hand can rein the rain—
　　No earthly power reigns o'er it.

15 May ——————————————————————

Jeremy lived in the land of A. He wanted to reach Palestine by adding a letter to A to make a familiar two-letter word, and then a letter to the two-letter word to make a familiar three-letter word, and so on until he reached the nine-letter word PALESTINE. Sometimes he mixed the letters up on purpose. This is how he did it:

He began with the A.
He added an N to make AN.
And a P to make PAN.
And an S to make SPAN.
And a T to make PANTS.
And an L to make PLANTS.
And an E to make PLANETS.
And an I to make PLAINEST.
And an E to make—PALESTINE!

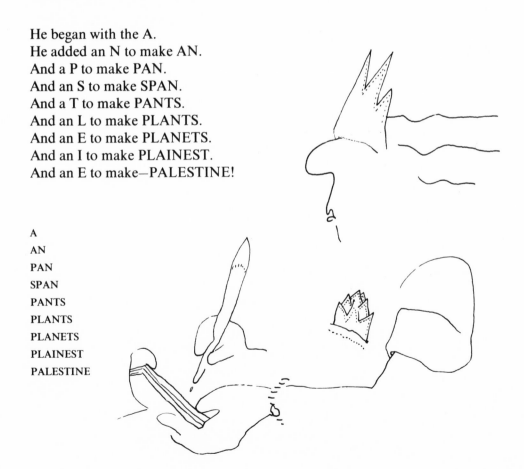

A
AN
PAN
SPAN
PANTS
PLANTS
PLANETS
PLAINEST
PALESTINE

16 May————————————————

HAVING TOO MUCH FUN

Having too much fun
On MON.
Will induce the blues
On TUES.
You take to your bed
On WED.
And your vision blurs
On THURS.
Then alas you die
On FRI.
And are buried flat
On SAT.
(You should have had your fun
On SUN.)

—W.R.E.

17 May————————————————

Excuse My Red Face

Announcers on radio and television made these bloopers:

- Reading a commercial for Ruppert's Beer, the announcer said, "When you want to relax after a hard day's work, try Buppert's Rear."

- And: "Your kids will love delicious M & M candies. They melt in your hand—not in your mouth!"

- And again: "At Moe's Esso Station, you can get gassed, charged up, and your parts lubricated in thirty minutes!"

- And: "Steinberg's Department Store has just received a shipment of large-size bathing suits. Ladies, now you can buy a bathing suit for a ridiculous figure."

- And: "And for all you kiddies, we are going to dish out cherry ice cream on today's program in celebration of today, February 22, George Birthington's Washday!"

- And: "Here is the weather report: Tomorrow roudy followed by clain."

18 May

"I'm Dying," He Croaked

In the sentence *"I'm dying," he croaked,* "croaked" is a pun because it means both "died" and "made a low, hoarse sound." In *"Bad shooting," the hunter groused,* "groused" is a pun because "groused" means "complained," but the hunter was after *grouse.* The Tom Swifties you saw earlier used *adverbs* to pun with; those you have just read pun with *verbs* instead. Roy Bongartz, who invented this kind of Tom Swifty, calls them *croakers.* Here are more of them:

- "You can't really train a beagle," he *dog*matized.
- "That's no beagle, it's a mongrel," she *mutt*ered.
- "You ought to see a psychiatrist," he re*mind*ed me.
- "That's my gold mine!" he *claim*ed.
- "But it was mine!" he ex*claim*ed.
- "And I used to be a pilot," he ex*plain*ed.
- "The fire is going out," he *bellow*ed.
- "Another plate of steamers all around," he *clam*ored.

Mr. Bongartz also has devised double-worded croakers:

- "I've got a new game," *mumbled Peg.*
- "My bicycle wheel is melting," he *spoke soft*ly.

19 May

Some words are difficult to rhyme, and others cannot be rhymed at all without playing tricks, such as splitting a word, or rhyming one word with two or three, or making a new word. These rhymes were difficult to arrange:

SILVER

To find a rhyme for silver
Or any "rhymeless" rhyme
Requires only will, ver-
bosity,* and time.

—STEPHEN SONDHEIM

VELOCITY

Having once gained the summit and managed
to cross it, he
Rolls down the side with uncommon velocity.

—R. H. BARHAM

If a masculine porker's a he-onk,
The feminine must be a she-onk;
When the gal meets the guy
In a Long Island sty,
They're a he-onk and she-onk in Speonk.**

—W.R.E.

* Verbosity is when you use more words than you need to.

**Which is, as noted, a town in Long Island (New York).

20 May

Some words are so long that I am sure no one ever pronounces them right.

Llanfairpwllgwyngyllgogerychwyrndrobwllllandysiogogogoch is the name of a small town in Wales. It means "The church of St. Mary in a hollow of white hazel, near to the rapid whirlpool, and to St. Tisilio church, near to a red cave." If you write to a friend there, put only the first twenty letters, Llanfairpwllgwyngyll, on the envelope; the post office will know what you mean.

Chargoggagoggmanchauggagoggchaubunaqwnaqungamangg is the Indian name of Lake Webster, in south-central Massachusetts. It means "I fish on my side, you fish on your side, nobody fish in the middle."

Chancellor Bismarck of Germany considered *apothecary* an insufficiently German word, and coined a seventy-one-letter replacement: *Gesundheitswiederherstellungsmitterzusammenmischungsuerhaltnisskundiger.*

It's all *supercalifragalisticexpialidocious*—super!—as Mary Poppins said in a Walt Disney motion picture.

THE PRESCRIPTION

Said the druggist: "I'll take some dimethyloximidomesoralamide
And I'll add just a dash of dimethylamidoazobenzaldehyde;
    But if these won't mix,
    I'll just have to fix
Up a big dose of trisodiumphlorogluclintricarboxlycide."

21 May

TBM = Three Blind Mice, for Instance

A word made up of the initial letters of several words—WAC for a member of the *Women's Army Corps*, for instance—is an *acronym*. ASITSN is an acronym for "A stitch in time saves nine." ABITHIWTITB is an acronym for "A bird in the hand is worth two in the bush."

Elliott made the following acronyms from the first lines of nursery rhymes. See how long it takes you to identify the lines.

1. OMHWTTCTGHPDAB
2. DDDMSJ
3. TWALMAHHALG
4. WWWRTTT
5. SSMAPGTTF

22 May

Love and Sabotage

Alexander won a set of tennis from me today—most of the games went fifteen-love, thirty-love, forty-love when he was serving, and love-fifteen, love-thirty, love-forty when I was serving.

"Why do tennis players say 'love' for a zero score, Pop?" he asked afterward.

"The word isn't really *love* at all," I said. "Do you remember what I told you about hobson-jobsons—foreign words that change in English so that they sound like common English words? *Love* in tennis is a hobson-jobson. It is the way the English pronounced *l'oeuf*—'egg'—that is, zero, or nothing.

"And, by the way," I went on (trying to prove that I knew more than he did, even if he could beat me at tennis), "let me tell you the story of another word we borrowed from the French. It starts with the struggles, long before the French Revolution, between the nobles and the peasants, whom they mistreated miserably. The peasants fought back by stamping the nobles' newly planted fields with their wooden shoes to keep the seeds from sprouting. And they wrecked textile mills by throwing their shoes into the machinery.

"*Sabots* is French for wooden shoes. So the damaging of machinery to stop production came to be called *sabotage,* and sabotage it remains in both French and English to this day."

23 May

THE SKATEBOARD
My daddy has bought me a skateboard;
    He tried it out first at the store.
And that is the reason why mommy
    Says daddy can't walk anymore.

        —W.R.E.

MY TV SET
My TV set is only four,
    And still too young to talk;
But when it scratches at the door,
    I take it for a walk.

        —W.R.E

"You'd better keep your eyes open tomorrow," said Jeremy.

"Why?" asked Medora.

"If you don't, you might bump into something."

LAWYER: Your uncle left you over five hundred clocks.

ELLIOTT: It will take a long time to wind up his estate, won't it?

ALEXANDER: Isn't it wonderful how the little chicks get out of their shells?

ELLIOTT: It is even more wonderful how they get in!

Taylor wandered off from a picnic in the country one day and a prisoner who had dug a tunnel to escape came out of the ground beside him. "I'm free," shouted the prisoner.

"I'm almost four," said Taylor.

Typewriter, Typewriter

The top line of letters on a typewriter reads QWERTYUIOP. A clever person noticed that you could make the word TYPEWRITER by drawing just on the letters in that line. Ilene Astrahan and Alex Gross went further. Using only those ten letters, they drew up a vocabulary of two hundred and fifty words, in which they wrote a lively story about a land called QWERT. Here are two verses in the QWERT language:

TYPEWRITER, TYPEWRITER

Typewriter, typewriter, typewriter, type:
Pour out your poetry, pour out your tripe.

—W.R.E.

WIPE YOUR EYE

Wipe your eye, your peeper, pet:
Wipe out worry—pirouette!

—W.R.E.

26 May ───────────────────────────

Also Ghoti

Ten words make up at least a fourth of our speaking and writing. They are *a, and, I, in, is, it, of, that, the, to.*

Ask your friends to carry on a conversation without using any of these words, and to pay you a penny each time one of the words slips in. You will soon be a penny millionaire.

Another trick—ask them to pronounce the letters GH-O-TI: *gh* as in *tough, o* as in *women,* and *ti* as in *motion.* What will they say?

They will say "fish."

27 May ───────────────────────────

There Was a Young Fellow Named Hall

I think I have said before that puns play on words that have more than one meaning or that sound like words with other meanings. At one point in the limerick below, for instance, fall and spring are seasons. But in the same five lines, a fall is a tumble and a spring is a flow of water.

> There was a young fellow named Hall
> Who fell in the spring in the fall.
> > 'Twould have been a sad thing
> > Had he died in the spring,
> But he didn't—he died in the fall.

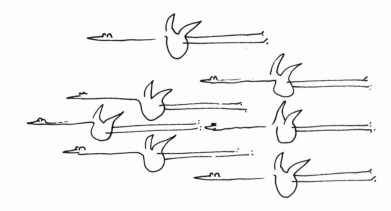

28 May

ALEXANDER: What are the two things you can't eat for breakfast?
ELLIOTT: Lunch and dinner.

JEREMY: I et six eggs for breakfast this morning.
ALEXANDER: You mean "ate," don't you?
JEREMY: Well, maybe it was eight I et.

MEDORA: Why don't you finish your alphabet soup, Jeremy? There are still
a few letters left.
JEREMY: I know, but they spell S-P-I-N-A-C-H!

The leopard settled back after supper and sighed contentedly: "Mm-
mmm-mmm! That hit just the right spots!"

29 May

The Half-Warmed Fish

Here are more spoonerisms—turned-around sounds—named after Dr. William Archibald Spooner, the man who said "blushing crow" when he meant
"crushing blow": What did he mean to say here?

- Calling on the dean of Christ Church, Spooner inquired, "Is the bean
  dizzy?"
- To a group of farmers, he began, "I have never before addressed so
  many tons of soil."
- Visiting a friend who had just acquired a country cottage, he congratulated him on his "nosey little cook."
- He hailed the "tearful chidings" of the gospels, and asked the congregation to sing with him "From Iceland's Greasy Mountains."

H. Allen Smith collected these spoonerisms:

- "I'm getting my soles half-shoed after I have a cough of cuppee."
- "The thot plickens."
- "The Indian died and went to the happy grunting hound."
- "Give me a jar of odorarm deunderant." ("That last item," says Mr.
  Smith, "is what I call a snooperism!")

BOBCATERPILLAR

Bobcaterpillar's umpteen feet
    are always spick and span and neat,
he sits and washes all day long,
    and sings his little washing song.
"Wash your eyebrows, wash your lashes,
    wash your byootiful moustaches,
wash each ear, and then, my dear,
    carefully wash behind that ear.
Am I head? Or am I tail—?
    Wash it all. And never fail
to scrub each toe and fingernail!"
    See him winding all about
almost turning inside out
    just to get at those umpteen feet,
and those hands, to keep them neat!

    Now he props his looking-glass
up against a blade of grass
    or a purple head of clover
there to look himself all over.
    "Am I spick? And am I span?
Preened and polished all I can?"
    And he's pleased, and purrs, and lifts
a teeny comb, and with it sifts
    one by one those lovely lashes
and those byootiful moustaches:
    combs each pointed little ear,
coils around to comb his rear,
    and—he's finished!—Well, what then?
Why, he'll wash it all again.
           —CONRAD AIKEN

31 May

Barbara, Hottentot

The ancient Greeks made fun of anyone who could not speak Greek; they said, "He just goes 'bar-bar.'" So they began calling foreigners *barbaros*, which is the source of our word *barbarian* (a rough, uncivilized person). Barbara, a very popular English given name, comes from *barbarian*.

————•————

When the Dutch landed on the Cape of Good Hope, at the southern tip of Africa, they could not make head nor tail of the native language, which seemed to consist largely of stammers. The only syllables the Dutch sailors could identify were *hot* and *tot*. So they called the natives Hottentots.

June

1 June

JUNE

When Jupiter wooed JUNO, in her ear
He hung the fairest month of all the year.
Right lovingly she thanked him for the boon,
And bussed him well, and called the jewel JUNE.

—W.R.E.

June's days are the longest of the year. You have scarcely turned the lights on in the evening when the sun comes up, and it is morning again:

YOU'VE NO NEED TO LIGHT A NIGHT LIGHT

You've no need to light a night light
On a light night like tonight,
For a night light's light's a slight light,
And tonight's a night that's light.
When a night's light, like tonight's light,
It is really not quite right
To light night lights with their slight lights
On a light night like tonight.

2 June

Take a Rain Check

A word that transfers its meaning to something quite different is called a metaphor. We use baseball terms every day, for instance, about things that have nothing to do with baseball. Here are a few examples:

He was born with two strikes against him.

Could you pinch-hit for me?

He couldn't get to first base with that girl.

He doesn't even know who's on first.

He sure threw me a curve that time.

I just call 'em as I see 'em.

I'll take a rain check on it.

He's only a bush leaguer.

He went to bat for me.

Major league all the way.

I liked him right off the bat.

We'll hit 'em where they ain't.

He was way out in left field on that one.

He was safe by a mile.

He's a foul ball.

He has a lot on the ball.

I think you're way off base on that.

He really dropped the ball that time.

Let's take a seventh-inning stretch.

We'll rally in the ninth.

I hope to touch all the bases on this report.

No games's ever lost until the last man's out.
　　　　　—JOHN O. HERBOLD II, *Verbatim*

And what means "to fail completely"? Why, says Mr. Herbold, what else but "strike out"?

3 June

Take season and seasoning,
Add them together,
And you'll spin through the air
As light as a feather.

Six letters form a holy word:
But swap the second and the third
And you'll be terrified, I've heard.

———•———

It's really easy, nothing to it:
Snip out this fish's second letter.
You'll leave behind a man to do it
(The snipping out) so much, much better.

———•———

I sit in fire, but not in the flame;
I follow the master, but not the dame;
I'm found in the church, but not in the steeple;
I belong to the monarch, but not to the people.

JARGON   4 June

Thieves used to talk to one another with secret words, so that the police would not know what they were saying. This kind of talk was called jargon, from an old French word meaning "twittering."

Jargon is still a specialized *in* language—musicians, scientists, and astronauts, for instance, have their own jargon. But generally when we say something is jargon we mean that it is full of big words with vague meanings, and awkward, dull sentences.

Still, some jargon is pretty lively. The users of citizens' band (CB) radio, many of whom are truck drivers, talk from car to car on the highway in terms like these:

- "What's your twenty?" (What's your location?)
- "Brush your teeth and comb your hair." (Be careful about the traffic rules—there's police radar ahead.)
- "Hammer off." (Slow down.)
- "Double nickel." (Fifty-five miles an hour, the national speed limit.)
- "A bear." (A policeman.)
- "Walk the dog." (Operate your CB radio set.)
- "Bear meat." (A speeding motorist.)

5 June———————————————

I WISH I LOVED THE HUMAN RACE

I wish I loved the Human Race;
I wish I loved its silly face;
I wish I liked the way it walks;
I wish I liked the way it talks;
And when I'm introduced to one
I wish I thought, "What jolly fun!"
—WALTER A. RALEIGH

6 June———————————————

But Who Is God's Brother?

Now that Alexander is twelve, he thinks a lot about sports like soccer and squash. But when he was only five or six, he thought a lot about God. Elliott, two years younger, was less interested in God than in having Alexander as a brother.

Once Alexander said, "Elliott, do you know that God is *everywhere*? God is love, and he is *everywhere*. He is even in your eyeball."

Elliott said, "But who is God's *brother*?"

Then Elliott got together with God too. He talked with him man to man. His mother heard him saying, "God, remember when we did visit your house? . . . God, do you bite just a little bit? . . . I think maybe you are a bird, God."

He even wrote him a letter. "Dear God," it went, "please send me some angles [he meant angels] and a box to keep them in."

Who ever heard of keeping angels in a box?

————•————

(The answer to Elliott's question about God's brother:)

POOR GOD

Got no father, got no mother—
How odd!
Hasn't even got a brother—
Poor God!
—W.R.E.

7 June

A woman who lived in Wausau
Had a lobster for daughter-in-law.
    She said, "Son, you're selfish,
    Withholding that shellfish:
Let's boil her, and each have a claw."

           —W.R.E.

If they ask, "Tilly hilly come ho,
Illy milly come rilly come ro?"
    I'll tell you at once
    Your proper response
Should be "Silly come willy come wo."

           —W.R.E.

8 June

The Surprising Number 37

The number 37 has a special magic to it.
If you multiply 37 × 3, you get   111.
If you multiply 37 × 6, you get   222.
If you multiply 37 × 9, you get   333.
If you multiply 37 × 12, you get   444.
If you multiply 37 × 15, you get   555.
If you multiply 37 × 18, you get   666.
If you multiply 37 × 21, you get   777.
If you multiply 37 × 24, you get   888.
If you multiply 37 × 27, you get   999.

9 June

Some words have little practical use, but are amusing because of their definition or curious background.

One is *sciapodous* (sigh-ap'-o-dus), which means "having large feet." The Sciapods were a semimythical tribe living near ancient Greece. Their feet were so large that they were used for umbrellas when it rained, and for parasols when the sun shone.

Then there is *qualtagh* (kwahl'-tahg). It is a Celtic word from the Isle of Man. What is a qualtagh? The first living thing you see on going out in the morning. Your qualtagh today may have been your dog, your brother or sister, your father or mother, or maybe a bird or a mouse.

10 June

The Ptarmigan

When Jeremy was just beginning to talk, he heard his brother Alexander practicing spelling aloud. In imitation, Jeremy began calling himself J-Jeremy, pronounced Jay-Jeremy. "Who spilled the juice?" his mother would ask; and his small voice would answer, "J-Jeremy did do it."

In some words, quite the other way from J-Jeremy, the first letter is not pronounced at all. In the far north, for instance, there lives a bird called the ptarmigan, with the *p* silent; the word is pronounced *tarmigan*. A writer whose name I do not know thought it would be amusing to put a *p* before other words that begin with a *t* sound, and wrote this verse:

> The ptarmigan is strange,
>   As strange as he can be;
> Never sits on ptelephone poles
>   Or roosts upon a ptree.
> And the way he ptakes pto spelling
>   Is the strangest thing pto me.

There are many words besides *ptarmigan* that start with a silent *p*. They come from the Greek language. *Psalm, psychology, pneumonia,* and *pterodactyl* are among them. Psurprising, pso to pspeak!

So the author could have placed a silent *p* before other words, and written his verse this way:

> The ptarmigan is pstrange,
>   As pstrange as he can be;
> Never psits on ptelephone poles
>   Or roosts upon a ptree.
> And the way he ptakes pto pspelling
>   Is the pstrangest thing pto me.

11 June⎯⎯⎯⎯⎯⎯⎯⎯⎯⎯⎯⎯⎯⎯⎯⎯⎯⎯⎯⎯

Joanna and Taylor

"Joanna," I said, "you are four years old now. Do you remember what you called your mommy when you first began to talk?"

"What?"

"You called her milk, because she had nursed you. You would look at her with an intent expression, and say, 'Mmm-ilk.' And you used to be a screamer. You screamed so loudly that Alexander and Elliott brought their friends over to hear you."

"I still do," said Joanna smugly.

I recall this conversation because it took place the same day I taught Joanna and Taylor—who, as usual, was wearing his Superman outfit—to play Knock Knock. This is the Knock Knock they learned:

JOANNA: Will you remember me in fifty years?
TAYLOR: Yes.
JOANNA: Will you remember me in twenty years?
TAYLOR: Yes.
JOANNA: Will you remember me next year?
TAYLOR: Yes.
JOANNA: Will you remember me next week?
TAYLOR: Yes.
JOANNA: Will you remember me in another minute?
TAYLOR: Yes.
JOANNA: Will you remember me in another second?
TAYLOR: Yes.
JOANNA: Knock knock.
TAYLOR: Who's there?
JOANNA: You forgot me already?

12 June⎯⎯⎯⎯⎯⎯⎯⎯⎯⎯⎯⎯⎯⎯⎯⎯⎯⎯⎯⎯

A Skunk Sat on a Stump

"Say this fast, and say it right, Pop," said Jeremy:

A skunk sat on a stump.
The skunk thunk the stump stunk,
But the stump thunk the skunk stunk.

I could not make it come out right.

13 June

Newspapers occasionally make funny mistakes in their headlines:

- Milk Drinkers Turn to Powder
- Shouting Match Ends Teacher's Hearing
- Scientists Are at Loss Due
  to Brain-eating Amoeba
- Dead Man Noted
  among Realtors
- New Orleans to Get Force of 50 State "Supersops"
- Woman Better after Being Thrown from High-rise
- Drunk Gets
  Nine Months
  in Violin Case
- Deer Kill 130,000
- Juvenile Court to Try
  Shooting Defendant

14 June

TO MLE

O, MLE, what XTC
I MN8 when UIC!
I used to rave of LN's II,
4 LC I gave countless sighs;
4 KT, and for LNR
I was a keen competitor;
But each now's a non-NTT,
4 UXL them all U C.
—LOUISE J. WALKER

15 June

Rose Bed

The headstone for John Rose and family reads

THIS GRAVE'S A BED OF ROSES

Other epitaphs from bygone days:

ON ARCHBISHOP POTTER
Alack, alack and well-a-day;
Potter himself is turned to clay.

ON A MUSIC TEACHER
Stephen and time
Are now both even:
Stephen beat time
Now time's beat Stephen.

ON EMMA AND MARIA LITTLEBOY
Two littleboys lie here.
Yet strange to say
The littleboys
Are girls.

ON MRS. NOTT
Nott born. Nott dead.
Nott christened.
Nott begot.
Lo here she lies
Who was
And who was Nott.

Nonsense Arithmetic, and so on

"Pop," said Alexander, "some of the limericks you write don't make much sense."

"They aren't supposed to make sense," I said. "They are supposed to be funny."

"But sometimes they aren't funny either," said Alexander.

That is the only trouble with my grandchildren—they have no respect. The two limericks below *do* make sense, whether they are funny or not. The first one throws a fresh light on arithmetic, and the second one throws a fresh light on spelling.

> Said a puzzled young pupil named Gunn,
> "Arithmetic's foolishly done.
> $\quad 2 \times 2 = 4$,
> $\quad$ So $\times$ = more;
> Yet 1×1 just = 1."
> $\qquad$ —W.R.E.

> A hungry young man from Poteetoo
> Decided to bite a moskeetoo;
> $\quad$ He said, "It is fit,
> $\quad$ Since I taste good to it,
> That it ought to taste good to meetoo."
> $\qquad$ —W.R.E.

Punctuate this verse so that it makes sense:

> Every lady in the land
> $\quad$ Has twenty nails on each hand
> Five and twenty on hands and feet
> $\quad$ This is true without deceit.

And this:

That that is is not that that is not that that is not is not that that is is not that it it is.

18 June

Mnemonics Is a Way to Remember

Some children, and more grown-ups, find it hard to remember. Usually it is because they don't pay enough attention in the first place. But there are tricks with words that can lock facts into your mind. Many people, for instance, remember to put their clocks ahead an hour in the spring for Daylight Saving Time, and back an hour in the fall for Standard Time, by saying to themselves, "*Spring* forward; *fall* back." They are using a trick that has a big name: *mnemonics.* It comes from Mnemosyne, a goddess of ancient Greece who was responsible for people's memory. (Do not pronounce the first *m* in *mnemonics* and *Mnemosyne;* say the words as if they started with an *n.*)

Jeremy's teacher told him he could remember how to spell *geography* by saying to himself, "George Eliot's Old Grandmother Rode A Pig Home Yesterday." Listed in order, the initial letters of the words spell *geography.* But Jeremy looked George Eliot up in the encyclopedia, and he says she had nothing to do with geography. She wrote novels.

19 June

JEREMY: Doctor, do you think raw oysters are healthy?
ALEXANDER: I never heard one complain.

JEREMY: How can Taylor stand behind Joanna and Joanna stand behind Taylor at the same time?
MEDORA: It's easy—they stand back to back.

ELLIOTT: Driver, what will you charge to take me to Beekman Place?
DRIVER: Three dollars for you, sir. Your baggage goes free.
ELLIOTT: Okay, then. You take the baggage, and I'll walk.

Charles Dickens caught the devil
  Stealing Charles Dickens's chickens!
"What the dickens?" cried the devil.
  "What the devil?" cried Charles Dickens.
—W.R.E.

There were two little radar sets,
  Each on a little ship;
And when the ships collided,
  The little sets went "Blip."

The Five Airy Creatures

Here is a riddle by Jonathan Swift, who wrote *Gulliver's Travels:*

We are little airy creatures,
All of different voice and features;
One of us in "glass" is set,
One of us you'll find in "jet,"
T'other you may see in "tin,"
And the fourth a "box" within.
If the fifth you should pursue,
It can never fly from "you."

22 June

Saxophone, Marmalade

Adolphe Sax, born in Belgium in the early nineteenth century, grew up accident prone: he was struck on the head by a brick, swallowed a needle, fell down a flight of stairs, toppled onto a burning stove, and accidentally drank sulfuric acid. None of this prevented him from perfecting, in 1835, a wind instrument combining the reed mouthpiece of a clarinet with a bent conical tube of metal, equipped with finger keys. In his honor, it is called the *saxophone.*

———•———

Marmalade—a pulpy jam of quince, plum, orange, or other fruit—is a popular breakfast spread with a name that has caused considerable confusion. One popular theory says it is an English corruption—another one of those hobson-jobsons—of *Marie Malade,* "sick Mary," because the jam, once a rarity, was among the few things that Mary Queen of Scots could hold in her stomach during an illness.

If anyone tells you that story, say it is not true. The name comes from *melimelon,* "honey apple," the Greek word for a quince.

23 June

The first italicized word in each line below ends in *s.* Add another *s,* and, as you see, it becomes an entirely different word.

MY S'S GROW S'S

My *s's* grow *s's, alas!"* cried *a lass;*
"My *handles* turn *handless,* my *bras* turn to *brass."*
A girl who *cares* deeply is quick to *caress;*
She dreams of the *posses* whose love she'd *possess;*
An *as* with an *s* is an *ass,* and no less,
When *asses* add *s's,* those *asses assess.*
Add *s's* to *mas* and they worship at *mass;*
Add *s's* to *pas,* and the *pas* make a *pass.*

—W .R.E.

114

24 June

Leotard, Ecdysiast

Do you go to dancing school? If so, you may practice in a *leotard*—a snug-fitting stretchy affair cut low in the neck. The word looks as if it should rhyme with leopard, but it does not.

> Leotard
> Rhymes with lard.
> Leopard
> Rhymes with shepherd.
> —W.R.E.

The leotard is named after the nineteenth-century tightrope walker who invented it—Jules Leotard.

———•———

A striptease is a special kind of dance in which the dancer takes off most of her clothes. I am glad to say that it is not generally taught in schools. Georgia Southern, a celebrated stripteaser, thought she should have a more dignified-sounding title than stripteaser, and asked the language expert H. L. Mencken to invent a substitute. Mencken proposed *ecdysiast* and the word quickly caught on. It comes from the Greek *ecdysis*. Ecdysis is what happens to a snake when it sheds its skin. Do you think it is a good description of a stripteaser?

25 June

You're Out!

"Tell me this, Pop," said Elliott. "If you were shut up in an iron house with no windows, no doors, and no other openings, not even a chimney, and you had nothing with you but a baseball bat, how would you get out?"

"Break down the walls with the bat," I said.

"You can't break an iron wall with a baseball bat," said Elliott scornfully. "Don't you know how to play baseball? Anybody could get out if he knew how to play baseball."

"I give up," I said.

"It's simple, Pop. Three strikes and you're out."

THE LONG SOUGHT-AFTER PROOF
THAT MONEY GROWS ON TREES

1. Money is what people get when they sell.
2. Sell sounds the same as cell.
3. A cell is a tiny room.
4. One kind of person who lives in a tiny room is a monk.
5. Monk is a short form of monkey.
6. Monkeys eat bananas.
7. Bananas grow on trees.
    THEREFORE, money grows on trees.
    —LOUIS PHILLIPS

NONSENSE **26 June**———————————————————

I SAW ESAU

I saw Esau kissing Kate.
Fact is, we all three saw.
I saw Esau, he saw me,
And she saw I saw Esau.

SHUT THE SHUTTER

"Go, my son, and shut the shutter,"
This I heard a mother utter.
"Shutter's shut," the boy did mutter,
"I can't shut 'er any shutter."

NAMES **27 June**———————————————————

"I'm eleven years old," writes Christine Loya. "I decided for extra credit to make up an alphabet poem based on girls' names. Would you write back and tell me if you like it?"

I like it.

A POEM OF GIRLS' NAMES

Abigail, Adeline, Alberta,
Bernadette, Holly, Dolly, Ada,
Cherly, Carolyn, Charlotte, Fay,
Diane, Deborah, Donna, Kay,
Elizabeth, Iris, and Darleen,
Francine, Emily, Kate, Kathleen,
Gertrude, Gilda, Faye, Irene,
Heather, Rhoda, and Helene,

Isabel, Iris, and Christina,
Jeannie, Julie, Joyce, Janina,
Karen, Kim, Kitty, Adella,
Lisa, Leslie, Linda, Laura,
Michele, Melinda, Martha, Maureen,
Nora, Nancy, Nicole, Noreen,
Otille, Ruth, Trixie, Olympia,
Patty, Pearl, Peggy, Patricia,
Queenie, Phyllis, Debbie, Suzanne,
Rita, Sharon, Mandy, Rosanne,
Sandy, Sybil, Sally, Susie,
Tammy, Liza, Tracy, Trudy,
Ursula, Dawn, Undine, Uraina,
Virginia, Viv, Val, Victoria,
Wilma, Stephanie, Wendy, Wanda,
Xavia, Bonnie, Kim, and Brenda,
Yvonne, Robin, Jane, and Joanie,
Zenobia, Alva, Faith, and Rosie.
—CHRISTINE LOYA

28 June ——————————————————————— PUNS

Problems at School

Elliott has attended several schools, and he says that in all of them the principals and the faculty members have had retirement problems.

When the principals retire they lose their faculties.

When the faculties retire they lose their principals.

Those are not new puns, but at least Elliott made them on purpose. The schoolboy who wrote the pun below punned by accident; his pun on vowels is really a malapropism.

The human body is divided into three parts: the Brainium, the Borax, and the Abominable Cavity. The Brainium contains the Brain. The Borax contains the Lungs, the Liver, and the Living Things. The Abominable Cavity contains the Bowels, of which there are five: A, E, I, O, and U.

29 June———————————————————————————

CHILD'S SONG

I have a garden of my own,
    Shining with flowers of every hue;
I loved it dearly while alone,
    But I shall love it more with you:
And there the golden bees shall come,
    In summer-time at break of morn,
And wake us with their busy hum
    Around the Siha's fragrant thorn.

I have a fawn from Aden's land,
    On leafy buds and berries nurst;
And you shall feed him from your hand,
    Though he may start with fear at first.
And I will lead you where he lies
    For shelter from the noon-tide heat;
And you may touch his sleeping eyes,
    And feel his little silvery feet.
           —THOMAS MOORE

30 June———————————————————————————

"I bet I can jump higher than a house," said Elliott.
    "I bet you can't," said Medora.
    "Of course I can. Did you ever see a house jump?"

    "I bet you can't stick your tongue out and touch your nose, Taylor," said Medora.
    Taylor tried and couldn't.
    "I'll show you how," said Medora.
    She stuck out her tongue and touched her nose with her finger.

    "What is the difference between a cat and a comma?" asked Alexander.
    "I don't know," said Jeremy.
    "A cat has its claws at the end of its paws, and a comma has its pause at the end of a clause," said Alexander.
    "What is the difference between a big black cloud and a lion with a toothache?" asked Jeremy.
    "I don't know," said Alexander.
    "One pours with rain and the other roars with pain," said Jeremy.

July

1 July

*JULY**

You swore that you would love me
    Until the seas ran dry, dear.
You knew you never loved me—
    O why, O why JULY, dear?
                    —W.R.E.

THE LADY AND THE SWINE
There was a lady loved a swine;
    "Honey," said she,
"Pig-hog, wilt thou be mine?"
    "Oink," said he.

"I'll build for thee a silver sty,
    Honey," said she,
"And in it softly thou shalt lie."
    "Oink," said he.

"Pinned with a silver pin,
    Honey," said she,
"That you may go both out and in."
    "Oink," said he.

"When shall we two be wed,
    Honey?" said she.
"Oink, oink, oink," he said,
    And away went he.

*July is named after Julius Caesar (100–44 B.C.), the Roman general and statesman.

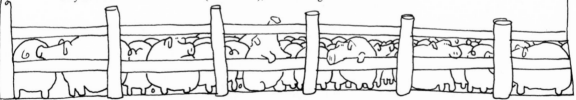

2 July

Spoonerisms, which you probably remember reverse sounds in speech, are sometimes intentional; the speaker is trying to be amusing. Those that follow, though, happened by accident.

1. Coffee always *weeps me a cake.*
2. (A speaker at a Fourth of July celebration): These *battle-scared* veterans—I mean these *bottle-scarred* veterans. . . .
3. Stephen Foster's immortal song, *Old Jack Blow.*
4. Fall is here; it's time for the *fleece to guy.*

What were the sentences supposed to say?

3 July

Lettuce Pray

If you hear the word *anguish,* you aren't likely to think it is *English.* And if you hear *languish* you aren't likely to think it is *language.* But if you hear someone saying "anguish languish" you might think he or she is saying "English language." A man named Howard Chace discovered you can tell whole stories, and have them understood, by replacing most of the words with words that sound a little bit like them but mean something entirely different. Anguish languish was the name he gave to this kind of wordplay. Here is the Lord's Prayer in Anguish languish:

> Hour Fodder wart unleavened,
> Hottub beehive mane.
> Tyke idiom crumb, Tie wilt bean numb,
> Inert acid dizzy emblem.
> Goofy dismay ordeal Libra head,
> Ant fig dinosaur deaths,
> Ass reefer keeper dentist.
> Leaners snot undo ten patients,
> Buddy liverwurst frumpy fill,
> Four thigh next seeking dumb,
> Deep powwow, auntie chlorine
> Fur river. Almond.
>   —MARK BURSTEIN

4 July

The Russians Have a Word for It

We declared our freedom from England on July 4, 1776, but we could not separate ourselves from the rest of the world, and we have to deal with people who speak languages we cannot understand at all. Translating from one language to another can be tricky, and is often wrong when it is done word for word. A Russian heard someone say, "The child was suspended for misconduct," and was shocked; the literal translation into Russian came out "The child was hanged for juvenile deliquency." Another time, a Russian tried to explain to an American girl that when he gazed on her lovely face time stood still; but what he actually said was, "You have a face that stops the clock."

During World War II, a Soviet diplomat complained to an American official that Washington was "behind" in delivering planes and tanks to Moscow. The American replied it was because Moscow was "behind" in letting us know what weapons they needed. "I have not come here," said the Russian, "to discuss my behind but your behind."

A Russian studied English day and night for ten years before he came to this country, and thought he knew the language perfectly. Then he visited New York and the first evening he was here, saw a sign outside a Broadway play that read: HAMLET PRONOUNCED SUCCESS. He gave up and went back home.

A Russian immigrant asked his neighbor: "You speak English, not so?" The neighbor replied: "A few, and then small."

5 July────────────────────────────

Eight in One

I know a word of only seven letters that contains eight other words—and you
can find them without changing the order of even a single letter.

The word is THEREIN. And the words inside are:

> the
> there
> he
> her
> here
> ere
> rein
> in

That is eight words in one. But you can add three more:

I

herein

re (the second sound in the scale: do, re, mi)

So really you have eleven words hidden away inside one seven-letter
word.

6 July────────────────────────────

Verses for Shouting

When Alexander, Elliott, and Jeremy are feeling especially lively, they
sometimes shout these two verses:

KING DAVID AND KING SOLOMON

> King David and King Solomon
>   Led merry, merry lives,
> With many, many lady friends,
>   And many, many wives.
> But when old age crept over them,
>   With many, many qualms,
> King Solomon wrote the Proverbs,
>   And King David wrote the psalms.
>   —JAMES BALL NAYLOR

THE ZOBO, ZEBU, YAK, AND BOBO

The Zobo is a cross between the Zebu and the Yak.
The Zebu has a dewlap, and a hump upon its back.
The Yak has hair that sweeps the ground. Don't
　　　mix these with the Bobo—
Which is a Mullet Fish, unlike the Zebu, Yak,
　　　or Zobo.

—W.R.E.

7 July ——————————————————————— **STORY**

How the King Found His Crown: I

When Medora was in the second grade, she wrote a story as a present for her mother. It is so exciting that I don't dare tell you all of it at once, so I will break it into pieces, just the way Medora wrote it. Here is the first piece:

*HOW THE KING FOUND HIS CROWN
BY MEDORA*

Chapter I: The king codent find his Crown

Once a pon a time there was a king who codent find
his Crown.
he was very sad. first he asked the Queen wer it was
I dont no she sed.
Then he asked the two prinsices.
No they sea we have not.
Then he went to see a nother king to see if he cood
borow his Crown.
no he said
can't I gust use it for one nite
no!! no!! no!!
sed the other king.
so the king who coodent find his crown went of sadlly.

—(To be continued on 7 August)

123

Burma Shave

"Tell us a story about the olden days, Pop," said Jeremy.

"Very well," I said. "In the olden days a company named Burma Shave advertised its shaving cream on road signs. They would put several signs along the highway, about a hundred feet apart, and when you had read them all you knew the verse. Like this:

Slow down, Pa
Sakes alive
Ma missed signs
Four and five

And

If harmony
Is what you crave
Then get a tuba
Burma Shave

And

Ben
Met Anna
Made a hit
Neglected beard
Ben-Anna split

"That's a pun, you see—on *banana* split."
"Pop, we aren't fools," said Elliott.
"Here is one more," I said:

My job is keeping
Faces clean
And nobody knows
De stubble I've seen.

"They are dreadful puns," said Medora.
But she laughed, all the same.

9 July

LONG WORDS

Padded Proverbs

Long words can be lots of fun to play with, and sometimes we need them to make a point very clear; but don't use fancy words just to show off. People who show off by fancy talk may think they sound superior, but they only sound silly. Nobody will admire you for saying "obese as a porcine young-ster" when what you mean is just "fat as a pig."

These four padded proverbs are filled with big, blown-up words. How do the real proverbs go?

1. Obstinate in the manner of the offspring of a horse and a donkey.
2. A small unit of monetary exchange retained equals that amount in wages.
3. The male human's most highly regarded follower is a canine.
4. A palmed fledgeling is equal in value to twice the number ob-scured in the underbrush.

10 July

LIMERICKS

A gentle old lion, alas,
Lay down with a lamb in the grass.
    The lamb ate the lion.
    (Hosannas to Zion!
If you believe that, you're an ass!)
        —W.R.E.

There was a forgetful old dame
Who won in a lottery game.
    The amount that was due
    Was a million or two,
But she couldn't remember her name.
        —W.R.E.

A corpulent person from Akt
Added pound upon pound as he snacked.
    Said his friends, "It is sad
    That although he can add,
He has never learned how to subtract."
        —W.R.E.

11 July

Dukes, Berserk

The duke of Wellington's nose compared in size to Pinocchio's. His troops called him "Nosey." Cockneys (people living in the East End of London, having a special dialect and accent) began to call noses "dukes" in his honor. Fists, which are used to punch people in the nose, were called "duke-busters." As time passed, "duke-buster" shrank back to "duke," but kept the meaning "fist." If you are told to "put up your dukes," you are being challenged to a fistfight.

————•————

A Norse hero of the eighth century was named Berserk for the *berserk* (bear skin) that he wore into battle. His twelve sons came to be known, with their father, as *Berserkers*. The name was then applied to a class of wild warriors who in battle howled like wolves or growled like bears, bit their shields, foamed at the mouth, and were dreaded for their enormous strength and apparent invulnerability. To go *berserk* is to go into a frenzy of rage.

12 July

Cricket ran a story by Donald Hall called "Riddle Rat." Here are some of Riddle Rat's riddles:

- What is the tiniest room in the world?
  The mushroom!

- Why does the silo stand beside the barn?
  It doesn't know how to sit down!

- What do you call a cat who weighs five hundred pounds, has six-inch-long teeth, and claws as sharp as razors?
  Sir or madam!

- What does a six-hundred-pound barn rat say?
  Here, kitty. Here, kitty.

ALEXANDER: What is white and has a peak and ears?
JOANNA: I don't know.
ALEXANDER: A snow-covered mountain.
JOANNA: But where are the ears?
ALEXANDER: Haven't you ever heard of mountaineers?

BAGPIPES

Puss came dancing out of a barn
With a pair of bagpipes under her arm;
She could sing nothing but Fiddle-cum-fee,
The mouse has married the humble-bee.
Pipe, cat—dance, mouse—
We'll have a wedding at our good house.

THE BOY STOOD ON THE BURNING DECK

The boy stood on the burning deck,
    His feet were full of blisters;
The flames came up and burned his pants,
    And now he wears his sister's.

Big Pig

Stinky pinkies, you recall, are definitions that rhyme:

- A fat hog is a   big pig.
- Colored lemonade is a   pink drink.
- Skinny James is   slim Jim
- A rabbit that makes you laugh is a   funny bunny.
- Foolish William is   silly Willy.
- A seafood platter is a   fish dish.
- A little frankfurter is a   teeny weenie.
- A good polish is a   fine shine.
- A corpulent puss is a   fat cat.
- A bad-tempered employer is a   cross boss.
- A tiny insect is a   wee bee.
- When the lights went out in Noah's boat, it was a   dark ark.

15 July————————————————

Drinking Song of a Hardhearted Landlord

This verse is easy to read if you simply count the number of syllables in each set that I have run together. Take ant-ant-ant-ant-ant-ant-ant-ant-ant-ant, for instance. Ten ants, right? Ten ants is *tenants,* right? Now go ahead.

Though my ant-ant-ant-ant-ant-ant-ant-ant-ant-ant a lass
    who's a loner,
So many con-der-der-der-der-der-der-der-der-der are milling
About with pre-tion-tion-tion-tion-tion-tion-tion-tion-tion to own her,
They'd be dear at ha'penny-ha'penny-ha-penny-ha'penny-ha'penny-
    ha'penny-ha'penny-ha'penny-ha'penny-ha'penny the shilling.

CHORUS: They'd be dear at, *etc.*

The dril-dril-dril-dril-dril-dril-dril-dril-dril-dril that
    frame her sweet forehead
Would merit niel-niel-niel-niel-niel-niel-niel-niel-niel-
    niel* a-tion-tion-tion-tion-tion-tion-tion-tion-tion-tion
But her ement-ement-ement-ement-ement-ement-ement-ement-
    ement-ement mine—and *I'*m horrid:
I jeer at romantic in-tion-tion-tion-tion-tion-tion-tion-tion-tion-tion.

CHORUS: I jeer at, etc.
If she der-der-der-der-der-der-der-der-der-der her payments
    I care not
How der-der-der-der-der-der-der-der-der-der this lass when
    unbent.
Treat ant-ant-ant-ant-ant-ant-ant-ant-ant-ant as human? I
    swear not:
Their dency-dency-dency-dency-dency-dency-dency-dency-dency-
    dency not to pay rent.

CHORUS: Their dency-, etc.
           —W.R.E.

*John Tenniel drew the original pictures for *Alice's Adventures in Wonderland.*

Pnlleeeessss

Elliott wrote the letters PNLLEEEESSSSS on a piece of paper and asked the other children to rearrange them to make a familiar word that means you can't sleep. Alexander was the only one who succeeded. Can you figure out the word?

You remember that words made by juggling the letters of other words are called anagrams. PNLLEEEESSSSS is not a true anagram word, since it is not a word at all. But the words listed below are anagrams, and elegant anagrams at that. An elegant anagram is one where changing the letters of a word (or words) around makes a second word (or words) describing the first. That is just what happens here.

- Arguments: Must anger
- The nudist colony: No untidy clothes
- Beverly Sills: Silvery Bells
- Moonlight: Thin gloom
- Is pity love?:   Positively!
- A sentence of death: Faces one at the end
- Endearments: Tender names
- Panties: A "step-in"

IN THE BIG ROCK CANDY MOUNTAIN

In the big rock candy mountain
    All the cops have wooden legs,
And the bulldogs all have rubber teeth,
    And the hens lay hard-boiled eggs;
The farmers' trees are full of fruit,
    The barns are full of hay;
Oh, I'm bound to go where there ain't no snow,
Where the rain don't fall and the wind don't blow,
In the big rock candy mountain.
    Oh, the buzzin' of the bees. . . .

In the big rock candy mountain
    You never change your socks;
And the little streams of alkyhol
    Come a-tricklin' down the rocks;
The jails they all are made of tin,
    The railroad bulls are blind;
There's a lake of stew, and whiskey too,
You can paddle all around in a big canoe,
In the big rock candy mountain.
    Oh, the buzzin' of the bees. . . .

JUMBLED GEOG- RAPHY   # 18 July————————————————

GEOGRAPHICAL LOVE SONG

In the state of Mass.
There lives a lass
    I love to go N.C.;
No other Miss.
Can e'er, I Wis.,
    Be half so dear to Me.

R.I. is blue
And her cheeks the hue
    Of shells where waters swash;
On her pink-white phiz
There has Nev. Ariz.
    The least complexion Wash.

La! could I win
The heart of Minn.,
    I'd ask for nothing more;
But I only dream
Upon the theme,
    And Conn. it o'er and Ore.

Hawaii, pray,
Can't I Ala.
    This love that makes me Ill.:
N.Y., Oh., Wy.
Kan. Nev. Ver. I
    Propose to her my will?

I shun the task
'Twould be to ask
    This gentle maid to wed.
And so, to press
My suit, I guess
    Alaska Pa. instead.

19 July———————————————— PUSH-BUTTON TUNES

Did you know that you could play tunes by pushing the buttons on a push-button telephone? It's a fact. All you need to do is call a friend, and then dial (*after* your friend is on the phone*) like this:

ROW, ROW, ROW YOUR BOAT

Row, row, row your boat
4   4   4   8   6
Gent-ly down the stream
6   2   6   9   #
Mer-ri-ly mer-ri-ly
0 0 0
Mer-ri-ly mer-ri-ly
* * * 4 4 4
Life is but a dream.
6 2 2 1   1

LONDON BRIDGE

Lon-don Bridge is fall-ing down
6   9   6   8   7   8   6
Fall-ing down fall-ing down
1   4   5   7   8   9
Lon-don Bridge is fall-ing down
6   9   6   8   7   8   6
My fair la-dy.
8   6   0   4

*Don't push the buttons to make a tune before you have someone on the other end of the line. You may get a long-distance number by mistake.

131

20 July

The Mrs. Kr. Mr.

If Mr. is pronounced mister, why shouldn't "kissed her" be shortened to "kr.," and "blister" to "blr.," and so on? If "Mrs." is pronounced "missus," why shouldn't "kisses" be shortened to "krs."? Let us try and see what happens.

> *THE MRS. KR. MR.*
>
> The Mrs. kr. Mr.
> Then how her Mr. kr.!
> He kr. kr. kr.
> Until he raised a blr.
> The blr. killed his Mrs.
> Then how he mr. krs.!
> He mr. mr. mr.
> Until he kr. sr.
> He covered her with krs.
> Till she became his Mrs.
> The Mrs. kr. Mr.
> (and so on and on and on)
>
> —W.R.E.

21 July

Disemvoweled Proverbs

Medora found these word puzzles in a book.

Just follow the instructions, and each of the lines below will turn into a proverb. (Suppose, for instance, you are asked to insert the letter *O* four times in ARLLINGSTNEGATHERSNMSS. This is where you would put them: AR*O*LLINGST*O*NEGATHERSN*O*M*O*SS—that is, "A rolling stone gathers no moss.")

1. Insert the letter *I* four times in ASTTCHNTMESAVESNNE.
2. Insert the letter *I* four times in ABRDNTHEHANDSWORTH TWONTHEBUSH.
3. Insert the letter *O* three times in GFURTHERANDDWRSE.

4. Insert the letter *A* nine times in ERLYTOBEDNDERLYTORISE-MKESMNHELTHYWELTHYNDWISE.
5. Insert the letter *E* five times in BTTRLATTHANNVR.
6. Insert the letter *E* three times in ALLSWLLTHATNDSWLL.

22 July ————————————————

The Word Don't Mean What You Think It Does

Give the meaning of

> 0
> M.D.
> B.A.
> D.D.S.
> M.A.
> Ph.D.

"That's easy," says Alexander. "It's 'five degrees below zero.'"
Give the meaning of

> C
> O
> N

"That's easy," says Elliott. "It's 'condescending.'"

23 July ————————————————

Boycott

Back in 1880 the earl of Erne, an Englishman who owned tens of thousands of acres in County Mayo, Ireland, sent Captain C. C. Boycott to collect rent from the tenants who farmed the land. The harvest had been disastrous, and the tenants had no money. They could not even pay in grain, since they had no grain. But Captain Boycott refused to postpone the payments or to reduce the rents. He tried to throw the tenants off the land by force. At last they ganged up on him. Nobody would sell him food. All the servants left, down to the last stable boy. They made life so miserable for him that he gave up and returned to England.

This kind of joint protest, in which people try to change the policies of individuals or companies or governments by refusing to do business with them, has been known ever since as a *boycott*.

NONSENSE   ## 24 July

I never had a piece of toast
    Particularly long and wide,
But fell upon the dirty floor,
    And always on the buttered side.

—JAMES PAYNE

The hen it is a noble beast
The cow is more forlorner
Standing in the rain
With a leg at every corner.

Good and Not so Good

"I want to be altogether good," said Alexander.

"I want to be altogether bad," said Medora. (But she didn't mean it.)

"There is no such thing as altogether good or bad," I said.

"Oh yes there is," said Medora.

"I will prove I am right," I said. "Listen to this old story. Two pilots went up in an airplane. The airplane had a motor."

"That's good," said Elliott.

"No, that's bad. The motor didn't work."

"That's bad," said Medora.

"No, that was good. They had a parachute."

"Oh, that's good," said Elliott.

"No, that was bad," I said. "The parachute didn't open."

"Yes, that was bad," said Medora.

"No, that was good," I said. "There was a haystack under them."

"Oh, that's good," said Elliott.

"No, that was bad," said I. "There was a pitchfork in the haystack."

"That's bad," said Medora.

"No," said I, "that's good. They missed the pitchfork."

"That's good," said Elliott.

"No, that was bad," I said. "They missed the haystack too."

Said daddy one night when well-oiled,
"My girls are too sweet to be spoiled.
   I dote on their tresses,
   Their dimples, and dresses;
They'd taste simply marvelous broiled."
—W.R.E.

A man caught a magical fish.
Said the fish, "I will grant you one wish."
   Said the man, "You are kind;
   I hope you won't mind
Being trout amandine on a dish."
—W.R.E.

27 July

You Should Have Washed

Medora's jokes may seem funnier to me than they really are because her high forehead appears so serene and her wide-set gray eyes so innocent when she tells them. But they are not truly innocent at all.

"Add these up," she said this morning to Alexander.
"Add what up?"
"One ton of sawdust."
"All right."
"One ton of old newspaper."
"All right."
"Ten tons of string."
"All right."
"And a half a ton of bones. Have you got all that in your head?"
"Yes," said Alexander.
"I thought so," said Medora.

"Did you get wet today?" she asked Jeremy.
"No," said Jeremy.
"You should have washed," said Medora.

28 July

Use Any Vowel

If you replace the *A* in the words listed below with any of the other vowels—*E, I, O,* or *U*—you will still have a perfectly good word:

- Bag: Beg, big, bog, bug
- Ball: Bell, bill, boll, bull
- Blander: Blender, blinder, blonder, blunder
- Last: Lest, list, lost, lust
- Mass: Mess, miss, moss, muss
- Pack: Peck, pick, pock, puck
- Pat: Pet, pit, pot, put

Cinderella,
Dressed in yella,
Went downtown
To buy some mustard;
On the way
Her girdle busted—
How many people
Were disgusted?
One, two, three, four, five, six. . . .

———•———

Fatty on the ocean
    Fatty on the sea
Fatty broke a bottle of milk
    And blamed it on me.
How many whippings did he get?
    One, two, three, four, five . .

30 July —————————————————————— RIDDLES

Can you name the capital of all the states in just thirty seconds?
Of course—Washington, D.C.

How many bushel baskets full of earth can you take out of a hole two feet wide and two feet deep?
None. The earth has already been taken out.

What is the difference between an elephant and a flea?
An elephant can have fleas, but a flea can't have elephants.

What makes the Tower of Pisa lean?
It doesn't eat enough.

Tell me now
What is it that
Is over your head
And under your hat?
Your hair.

—ENNIS REES

With which hand
Now you tell me,
Should you stir
Your cup of tea?
With neither—most people use a spoon.

—ENNIS REES

If you answer this
I'll be fit to be tied:
Which side of a pie
Is the left side?
The side that isn't eaten.

—ENNIS REES

ONOMATO-
POEIA

31 July

On May 3 I talked about *onomatopoeia,* which means words that imitate sounds—bow-wow for the bark of a dog, for instance, or cock-a-doodle-do for the crow of a rooster. Here are more words like that:

1. Crack, whip!
   Train, chuff!
   Jog, horse!
   Puff-puff!

2. Babble, brook!
   Fountain, splash!
   Trickle, faucet!
   Drip, wash!

3. Buzz, saw!
   Stick, glue!
   Hoot, train!
   Choo-choo!

4. Baa, sheep!
   Moo, cow!
   Croak, frog!
   (Bow-wow!)

5. Bell, ring,
   Ding-dong!
   (Gun: BANG!
   End of song.)

—W.R.E.

August

1 August

*AUGUST**

We are sweatiest
Which makes us wettiest
And soggiest
In Augiust.

—W.R.E.

TO MY ITSY-BITSY LOVEY-DOVEY

You and I will have a powwow;
I'll say mishmash, you'll say bow-wow;
We will visit in Columbo,
We will talk in mumbo jumbo;
I'll have clothes that raggle-taggle,
You'll have teeth that sniggle-snaggle;
In Japan we'll stop a fairy
From committing hari-kari;
When we tingle, we will tangle,
We will jingle, we will jangle;
In a quiet little alley
You and I will shilly-shally;
You will call me silly Billy,
I will kiss you willy-nilly;
All the day we'll dillydally,
I will call you silly Sally;
When you weep into your hanky,
We will stop our hanky-panky.

—W.R.E.

*Named for Augustus (63 B.C.–A.D. 14), first Roman emperor.

2 August

TEACHER: Jeremy, this homework looks like your mother's handwriting!
JEREMY: Yes, teacher—I used her fountain pen.

TEACHER: If you have eleven potatoes and have to divide them equally among five people, how would you do it?
ALEXANDER: I'd mash them.

ELLIOTT: Teacher, I don't deserve zero on this paper!
TEACHER: I know, but it is the lowest mark I can give you.

TEACHER: Medora, what is a synonym?
MEDORA: A synonym is a word you use when you can't spell the other one.

TEACHER: I hope I didn't see you looking at Alexander's book, Jeremy.
JEREMY: I hope so too, teacher!

3 August

Say It Again, Sam

Musical instruments that make a continuous sound double or treble their names in many countries. I do not know what most of the following instruments are, but I like to read the list aloud; it sounds like a Javanese orchestra warming up for a gig. Try it.

STRINGS

Adeudeu · chi-chu · dongeldongel · gendang-gendang · geso-geso · gettun-gettun · git-git · gobi-gobi · hum-strum · hu hu · iqliq · jigi-jigi · kandiri-kandire · keteng-keteng · kimwanyewanye · klung-klung · kolong-kolong · ogung-ogung bulu · setsegetsege · tangge tong · tingning · ton-ton · yang kong.

WINDS

Asukusuk · bumbun · burumamaramu · cuckoo · damyadamayan · dge-glie · elo-ilo-goto · empet-empetan · fango-fango · going-going · huayra-puhura · iyup-iyup · kio-kio · kivudi-vudi · mero-mero · noli-noli · om-om · ower-ower · pib-pib · pi-pi · poti-poti · putura-putura · puwi-puwi · remo-remo · trutruka · tutu · ufu-ufu · wer-wer.

PERCUSSION

Agogo • angang-angang • asakasaka • atata-witata • baka-baka • banga-banga • budubuduke • bum-bum • buruburu • chacha • chaingvaing • chal-chal • cheng-cheng • chullo-chullo • ciocca-ciocca • cupa-cupa • dabdaba • daola-daola • degangangde • didimbadimba • dingdingti • dog-dog • doli-doli • dugdugi • dundun • gah-gah • ganga-ganga • gangan • gew-gaw • ghun-ghuna • gom-gom • gong-ageng • gong-angang-angang • gua-gua • gubgubi • gudu-gudu • gue-gue • gul-gul • huli-huli • jhanjhana • joucoujou • jul-jul • ka-eke-eke • kakanika-kanika • kao-kao • kemkem • kentung-kentung • keri-keri • kingulu-ngulu • kinkinki • knicky-knackers • konkon • kritsa-kritsa • kul-kul • lae-lae • ore-ore • pangang • patpati • pim-pim • pong-pong • qalqal • qemqem • rau-rau • reco-reco • re-re • reso-reso • rigu-ragu • saga-saga • saing waing • sake-sake • sanbamba • sege-sege • seke-seke • shak-shak • sil-sil • sung-chung • tabang-tabang • tamatama • tambattam • tam-tam • tantan • temettama • tepan-tepan • tintinnus • tin tin sags • to-ko • tom-tom • tong-gong • tong-tong • wongang • wupu-wupu • xaque-xaque • yangong.

—HARRY RANDALL

4 August————————————————

Blest Be That Beast

I have told you about homonyms—words that are the same in sound, and sometimes in spelling, but are different in meaning. Using the clues, guess the homonyms in the verses below.

I found a shaggy mare in (1)——.
With might and (2)—— I trimmed her (3)——.

Clues: 1. An American state 2. Physical strength
3. Long hair

Say, (1)—— man in thy (2)—— cot,
Art (3)—— with thy lowly lot?

Clues: 1. Saintly 2. Full of holes 3. Altogether

I met a wise antelope, born in a zoo;
But I couldn't find out what that (1)—— (2)—— (3)——.

Clues: 1. Opposite of old 2. Kind of antelope
3. Past tense of know

141

5 August

HAPPY BIRTHDAY, TAYLOR!

In Mobile Bay upon this day in 1864,
Came Farragut a-storming up before the forts on shore.
He laughed at the torpedoes, and he cried, "Full speed
    ahead!"*
(And Taylor's mother tells me that is just what *Taylor*
    said
The very instant he was born—on August 5, the day
That Farragut so long before had stormed up Mobile Bay.)

—W.R.E.

*In the War Between the States, Admiral Farragut commanded a fleet that steamed through the minefields in Mobile Bay and forced the surrender of the Confederate forts guarding the bay. Mines at that time were called torpedoes. After Farragut's leading ship had been sunk by a mine, he exclaimed, "Damn the torpedoes! Full speed ahead!"

6 August

Stuff and Nonsense!

IN WHAT WAYS ARE A VIOLIN AND A BOOKCASE ALIKE?

Across

1 "Oh, say, _____ you see . . ."
4 Large passenger vehicle that follows a street or road route
7 Additional amount
8 Subject (rhymes with "tropic")
10 Against; opposed to
11 Initials of Horatio Nelson
12 Plural (abbreviation)
14 Poor grade, below average
15 A bird may build its nest in this
17 Exists
18 Sing with closed lips
19 Nickname for Timothy
21 Single article; bit of news

23 Use a brush and _____ to groom your hair
24 Neither here _____ there
25 Sound made by a sheep
26 Short way of saying "all right"
27 Floor pads for wrestling
28 First letter of the alphabet
29 A charge for services; doctor's _____
31 More _____ less
32 High in stature; not short
35 _____-in movie theater
37 Wicked
38 Had a meal
39 Knock

Down

1. Not in favor of; opposite of "pro"
2. Painting is one; so is sculpture
3. Not one or the other
4. Old Mother Hubbard went to fetch this for her dog
5. Opposite of "down"
6. Drink a little at a time
7. Angry; crazy
8. Him and her
9. Shinny up; clamber
13. You and me
16. "Yo-ho-ho, and a bottle of _____!"
19. Appliance for browning bread (rhymes with "roaster")
20. Contraction for "I am"
21. Colored with ink
22. "As I was going _____ St. Ives"
23. This pet belongs to the same family as the tiger
25. Like Old Mother Hubbard's cupboard
26. "My country, 'tis _____ thee"
27. Change position or place
28. "_____ the king's horses"
30. Historical period
33. Girl's name
34. Keep a stiff upper _____
36. That thing

(Answer to question in title:)

_ _ _ _ _ _   _ _ _ _   _ _ _   _ _ _ _
3 Down   26 Down 8 Down   1 Across 9 Down

_ _   _ _ _ _   _ _ _ _ _   _ _ _ _   _ _ _ _ _
28 Across 32 Across   15 Across   31 Across   35 Across

_ _   _ _ _ .
28 Across 4 Across.

—RUTH LAKE TEPPER

143

7 August———————————————————————————

*How the King Found His Crown: II**

Chapter II: The crown was in the cichen

the king had put his crown on the tabble while he was scraching his head. the cook had wanted to put on the crown. When the king left he put it on his head. the cook liked wering the crown. he wore it for a week when nowun was looking. Then one day wille he was stiring the soup it fell in but befor he new it was on the botum of the Boal before he cood get it owt the Watere toke the soup.

—(To be continued on 17 September)

*Medora's story continues from 7 July.

8 August———————————————————————————

Oh, Say Can You C

If you put a *c* before each capitalized word in this verse (not counting the pronoun I, or the words that begin the lines), the verse will begin to make sense (well, a little sense).

The upper Rust I All myself,
    A Hap with Ash to Row about;
I Lip poor Lucks of hard-earned pelf;**
    I'm Lever; I'm a At with Lout.

Though Ranks may Hide me, what Are I?
    I live in Lover; Reed I've none.
I Harm, I Heat, I also lie.
    A Rook I may be—but I'm fun.

As I Limb Loser to my Rest,
    Admit that I have Lass, old Hap.
Don't Luck at me—I do my best;
    I'm Lose to perfect. Why not Lap?

—W.R.E.

**Pelf means money—but people are more likely to speak of "ill-gotten" pelf than "hard-earned" pelf.

9 August ——————————————————————————————

PIG LATIN LOVE LYRIC

Elliott talks pig Latin; he takes the first letter of a word, transposes it to the back of the word, and adds "-ay": "Id-day ou-yay o-gay oo-tay cool-say ooday-tay?", for instance, means "Did you go to school today?" Jeremy's pig Latin is called Aragoo: he puts "arag" after the first letter of each word, or before the first letter of words that start with vowels. He says "Laragittle Jaragack Haragorner saragat aragin ara caragorner" for "Little Jack Horner sat in a corner." Alexander is taking first-year Latin now, and the code language he likes best adds Latin endings to English words. This is his favorite pig Latin verse:

> Lightibus outibus in a parlorum,
> Boyibus kissibus sweeti girlorum;
> Daddibus hearibus loudi smackorum,
> Comibus quickibus with a cluborum.
> Boyibus gettibus hardi spankorum,
> Landibus nextibus outside a doorum;
> Gettibus uppibus with a limporum,
> Swearibus kissibus girli nomorum.

10 August ——————————————————————————————

MEDORA: How do you make a cigarette lighter?
JEREMY: Take out the tobacco.

MEDORA: Do you entertain evil thoughts?
ALEXANDER: Oh, no—they entertain me.

MEDORA: Taylor's been walking since he was a year old!
JEREMY: Doesn't he ever get tired?

MEDORA: How can you get into so much mischief in one day?
ELLIOTT: Well, I get up earlier than most kids.

ALEXANDER: If the king of Russia was a czar and his wife was a czarina, what were their children?
JEREMY: Czardines.

11 August

Waltz, Nymph

"Alexander," I said, "your hair is in your eyes again."

His hair has been in his eyes almost since the day he was born. It is dark and thick and curly and hides his forehead. But it never quite manages to cover his eyes, which are big and dark and laughing. And, of course, it does not hide his huge grin.

He grinned now, looking up from his desk. "Pop," he said, "I am working on a pangram. Have you ever heard of pangrams?"

"Of course I have," I said. "A pangram is a sentence, or maybe more than one, that contains every letter in the alphabet. Wait a minute—I'll bring you one that I wrote before you were born."

I found it in my files. "It is called 'Peace in Our Time,' " I said, "and this is the way it goes:

> *God be his judge: that passive, zealous Quaker*
> *Who first yields Country; Kindred next; then Maker."*

He thought about it. "That's nice, Pop," he said, "but it's too easy. How many letters does it have?"

I counted. "Seventy-eight," I said.

"Well, gee, there are only twenty-six letters in the alphabet. I want to write a pangram that will use every letter just once."

"You have a lifetime job ahead," I said—"if you want your pangram to make sense, that is."

"*A quick brown fox jumps over the lazy dog* has just thirty-two letters," he said.

"I know—I used to practice that sentence when I was learning to type. But the shorter the pangram is, the harder it is to understand it. *Pack my bag with five dozen liquor jugs* is one of the best; it has only thirty-two letters. *Waltz, nymph, for quick jigs vex Bud* has only twenty-eight."

Later I located a twenty-six-letter pangram by Clement Wood that was reasonably intelligible, though it seems to me he fudged a little by using initials:

Mr. Jock, TV quiz Ph.D., bags few lynx.

To understand that you need to assume that Mr. Jock is a TV celebrity, an MC on a game show, who likes to hunt.

Alexander is still trying to work out a sentence of fewer than forty letters that includes every letter in the alphabet. Can you do it?

12 August

Cretin

We call a born idiot a *cretin*. The word has an origin that brings a lump to the throat. Hundreds of years ago, in the French Alpine valleys of Valoi and Savoy, lack of iodine in the water caused the birth of monsters.

> The idiot-children were particularly horrific, having immense heads and swollen necks, protruding tongues and furrowed foreheads; their intelligence was much lower than that of the brutes. Nonetheless, being human, they must possess immortal souls, which set them utterly apart from the brutes. So the good peasants reasoned. And in pity and tenderness, they gave to the veriest monster the name which was an affirmation of immortality; for having been baptized the creature was at least *un chrétien,** and in due course would inherit the Kingdom of Heaven.
>
> —JOHN MOORE

*Chrétien is French for Christian.

13 August

Alexander says this is an ABC verse, but I call it a numbers verse because it plays more with numbers than with letters of the alphabet:

TO A SICK FRIEND

I'm in a 10der mood 2 day,
    & feel poetic, 2;
4 fun I'll just —— off a line
    & send it off 2 U.

I'm sorry you've been 6 o long;
    Don't B disconsol8;
But bear your ills with 42de,
    & they won't seem so gr8.

14 August

Two morons joined the cavalry and got horses and couldn't tell them apart; so one said he would cut the mane off his. That was okay till it grew back in. So then the other said he would cut the tail off his, and that was okay till it grew back in. They decided to measure them by hands then, and the black horse was two hands higher than the white one.

The little moron wrote himself a letter and when asked what it said, replied, "I don't know; I won't get it until tomorrow."

The little moron said he was glad his mother had named him Willy 'cause all the kids at school called him that.

—COLLECTED BY HERBERT HALPERT

15 August

Tabloid, Smog, Panjandrum

Not many words have exact birthdays. Here are two that do.

A *tabloid* is a newspaper with small pages, many pictures, and, often, sensational stories. First, though, it was a pill. On 14 March 1884, the firm of Messrs. Burroughs, Wellcome & Company trademarked the term *tabloid* for a condensed medical tablet. Because the pills were so small, *tabloid* was soon used to describe newspapers of reduced size.

Smog is a familiar epithet for the dirty air that frequently hangs over cities. It was first used within a day or two of 1 July 1905. On 3 July the *London Globe* wrote: "The other day at a meeting of the Public Health Congress, Doctor Des Boueux did a public service in coining a new word for the London fog, which he referred to as 'smog,' a compound of 'smoke' and 'fog.' "

We know the year, but not the exact day, that the word *panjandrum,* meaning "a muckamuck, a person of high importance," was coined in a nonsense story by Samuel Foote. It was 1755. Here is the story:

So she went into the garden to cut a cabbage-leaf to make an apple pie, and at the same time a great she-bear came running up the street and popped its head into the shop. "What! No soap?" So he died, and she very imprudently married the barber. And there were present the Picninnies, the Joblillies, the Garyulies, and the Grand Panjandrum himself, with the little red button at top, and they all fell to playing the game of catch-as-catch-can till the gunpowder ran out at the heels of their boots.

16 August — MORE IRISH BULLS

- An Irishman whose nephew was entering the priesthood said, "I hope that I may live to hear you preach my funeral sermon."

- A poor Irishman offered an old saucepan for sale. His children inquired why he parted with it. "Ah, me honeys," he answered, "I would not be after parting with it but for a little money to buy something to put in it."

- "I was going," said an Irishman, "over Westminster Bridge the other day, and I met Pat Hewins. 'Hewins,' says I, 'how are you?' 'Pretty well,' says he, 'thank you, Donnelly.' 'Donnelly!' says I; 'That's not *my* name.' 'Faith, no more is mine Hewins,' says he. So we looked at each other again, and sure it turned out to be nayther of us."

17 August — EPITAPHS

ON LESLIE MOORE

Here lies what's left
Of Les Moore.
No Les
No more.

ON JONATHAN POUND

Here lies the body of Jonathan Pound,
Who was lost at sea and never found.

ON JOHN BUN

Here lies John Bun;
He was killed by a gun.
His name was not Bun, but Wood;
But Wood would not rhyme with gun, and Bun would.

SPELLING # 18 August

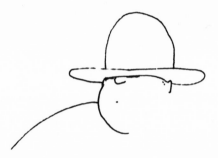

AN ORTHOGRAPHIC LAMENT

If an S and an I and an O and a U
    With an X at the end spell *Su;*
And an E and a Y and an E spell *I,*
    Pray, what is a speller to do?

Then, if also an S and an I and a G
    And an HED spell *side,*
There's nothing much left for a speller to do
    But to go commit *siouxeyesighed.*
        —CHARLES FOLLEN ADAMS

SPELLING SONG

Half of a swan,
        All of Eden,
That's the way
        To spell Sweden.
            —LOUIS PHILLIPS

A SLIP OR TWO # 19 August

Red Faces in Class

Elliott says he always knew that grown-ups make mistakes, but he is astonished to find that even schoolchildren are sometimes wrong. Many of their slips have been collected and put into books.

Alexander, Elliott, Medora, Jeremy, Joanna, and Taylor would never have made these slips:

150

- A mayor is a she horse.
- Quinine is the bark of a tree; canine is the bark of a dog.
- The animal which possesses the greatest attachment for man is woman.
- Vesuvius is a volcano and if you climb up to the top you will see the creator smoking.
- The plural of ox is oxygen.
- A yokel is the way people talk to each other in the Alps.
- Heredity means if your grandfather didn't have any children, then your father probably wouldn't have had any, and neither would you, probably.

20 August ——————————————— NONSENSE

A LOVE STORY

"What are you doing now, my pretty maid?"
"I'm going to sneeze, kind sir," she said.
"You ain't gonna sneeze at me, are you?"
"Yes, I'm going to sneeze," she said, "AT-CHEW!"
—WILLIAM COLE

ELVES' SONG

Buz! quoth the blue fly;
    Hum! quoth the bee:
Buz! and Hum! they cry,
    And so do we.
In his ear, in his nose,
    Thus do you see?
He ate the dormouse:
    Else it was he.
—BEN JONSON

21 August———————————————

- I'm an Indian, Tom said without reservation.
- I get up early, Tom said with alarm.
- I lost a fight with a lion, Tom said offhandedly.
- I'm a burglar, Tom broke in.
- I'm a double amputee, Tom said, defeated.
- How much is six and four, Tom asked tentatively.
- Step to the back of the boat, Tom said sternly.

—COLLECTED BY DAVID GOLDBERG

22 August———————————————

Edward Lear, who first made limericks famous, generally repeated the last word in the first line as the last word in the last line, as he did here:

> There was an Old Man with a beard,
> Who said, "It is just as I feared—
>   Two Owls and a Hen,
>   Four Larks and a Wren,
> Have all built their nests in my beard!"

Nowadays, however, the last line usually rhymes with the first two, as in these two famous examples:

> A diner while dining at Crewe
> Found a rather large mouse in his stew.
>   Said the waiter, "Don't shout
>   And wave it about,
> Or the rest will be wanting one too."

———•———

> There was an old man of Blackheath
> Who sat on his set of false teeth.
>   Said he, with a start,
>   "O, Lord bless my heart!
> I have bitten myself underneath!"

23 August

Punctuation can make a difference.
- Private—no swimming allowed!

does not mean the same as
- Private? No. Swimming allowed.

- The escaping convict dropped a bullet in his leg.

does not mean the same as
- The escaping convict dropped, a bullet in his leg.

- The butler stood by the door and called the guests' names.

does not mean the same as
- The butler stood by the door and called the guests names.

- Go slow, children.

does not mean the same as
- Go slow—children.

Nor does
- I'm sorry you can't come with us.

mean the same as
- I'm sorry. You can't come with us.

24 August

A flaky old fellow named Mark
Once said, "I've become Central Park—
　　Quite perfect for skating,
　　Or jogging, or dating,
But not very safe after dark."
　　　　　　—W.R.E.

A gunshot by accident pinked
The tail of a dodo, who winked,
　　And said, "If I cared,
　　I might have been scared;
But why should I care?—I'm extinct."
　　　　　　—W.R.E.

25 August

- Why do we say "scarce as hen's teeth?"
  Because hens have no teeth.

- Why do we say "to pull strings"?
  Because the puppeteer in a marionette show stands behind a curtain and pulls strings to make the puppets move.

- Why do we say "peter out"?
  Perhaps because, after the Romans seized Christ in the Garden of Gethsemane, Peter three times denied knowing his master. He "petered out."

- Why do we say "stark naked"?
  Stark comes from an old Anglo-Saxon word meaning "rump." Someone who is stark-naked is bare-rumped.

- Why do we say "straight from the horse's mouth"?
  Because the sure way to tell the age of a horse is to examine its teeth. "Straight from the horse's mouth" means from the highest authority—in this case, the horse itself.

26 August

Just Like Me

I played a joke on Taylor, and he hugged me and set off through the house on his battery-run scooter with the big tires to find Joanna and play the joke on her. He dodged around chairs and sofas and tables, never hitting one (though he looks like a Christmas card angel, with wide blue eyes and long tow hair, he has the quick reaction time of an athlete), shot down the long main hall, and found Joanna in her bedroom. I followed and listened:

TAYLOR: If I tell you a story, will you say, "Just like me" each time I stop?
JOANNA: I will.
TAYLOR: I went up a flight of stairs.
JOANNA: Just like me.
TAYLOR: I went up two flights of stairs.
JOANNA: Just like me.
TAYLOR: I went up three flights of stairs.
JOANNA: Just like me.
TAYLOR: I went into a little room.
JOANNA: Just like me.
TAYLOR: I looked out a window.
JOANNA: Just like me.
TAYLOR: I saw a monkey.
JOANNA: Just like me.
TAYLOR: JUST like YOU!

27 August ———————————————— NONSENSE

Moses supposes his toeses are roses,
But Moses supposes erroneously;
For nobody's toeses are posies of roses
As Moses supposes his toeses to be.

———•———

Johnny stole a penny once,
    And to the court was sent;
The judge found Johnny guilty,
    But he was in-a-cent.

———•———

The firefly is a funny bug,
    He hasn't any mind;
He blunders all the way through life
    With his headlight on behind.

28 August

Flying Wild

JEREMY: What makes you so sure that flying's safe?
ALEXANDER: If it wasn't, would they be letting you fly now, pay later?

The loudspeaker in the airport announced, "The plane for Seattle is now ready for its final departure."

"Well, I'm not," said Medora. "That's one plane *I'm* not going to take."

Alexander likes to tell this old joke. The other children come in on the chorus:

> The new automatic plane was making its first flight. A recorded announcement said: "This is the first all-automated jet. There is no pilot, no crew. Press a button and we take off. Press another button and dinner is served. Press another button and we land. Nothing can go wrong, can go wrong, can go . . ."

ALEXANDER: (At the airport) I wish we'd brought the television set.
ELLIOTT: Why?
ALEXANDER: I left the plane tickets on it.

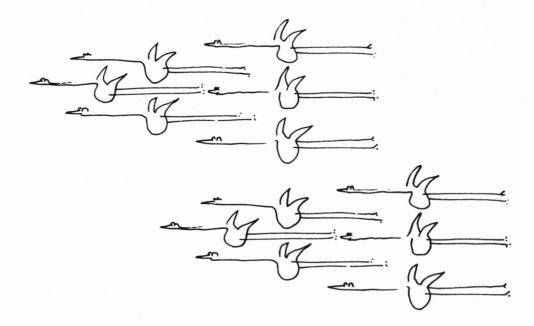

THE HORSES RUN AROUND

The horses run around,
Their feet are on the ground,
O who will wind the clocks when I'm away? (away)
Go get the ax,
There's a hair on baby's chin,
And a man's best friend is his mother (his mother)

While looking out a window,
A second-story window,
I slipped and sprained my eyebrow on the pavement;
    (the pavement)
Go get the Listerine,
Sister's got a beau,
And who cut the sleeves off Father's vest? (his vest)

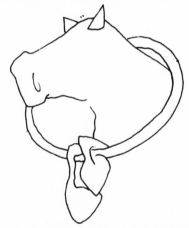

TWO LEGS BEHIND AND TWO BEFORE*

On mules we find two legs behind,
    And two we find before;
We stand behind before we find
    What the two behind be for.
When we're behind the two behind,
    We find what these be for;
So stand before the two behind,
    And behind the two before.

*Sung to the tune of *Auld Lang Syne.*

30 August

Words from Nowhere

People who specialize in studying the origin of words are called etymologists. They can tell you the history of almost every word in the language. But not all of the words. No one, for instance, knows where these words came from:

- Conniption (tantrum)
- Cub (the young of bears and certain other carnivorous animals)
- Culvert (a sewer or drain crossing under a road)
- Curmudgeon (a cantankerous person)
- Dander (temper)
- Dollop (a large helping)
- Larrup (to flog or thrash)
- Moniker (a personal name or nickname)
- Moola (money)
- Nincompoop (a blockhead)
- Tantrum (a conniption)

31 August

Not all Irish bulls are Irish. This one is from the city council of Canton, Mississippi:

> The following resolutions were passed: 1. Resolved, by this Council, that we build a new Jail. 2. Resolved, that the new Jail be built out of the materials of the old Jail. 3. Resolved, that the old Jail be used until the new Jail is finished.

George Selwyn, the missionary, once remarked that it seemed impossible for a lady to write a letter without adding a postscript. A lady present replied, "The next letter you receive from me, Mr. Selwyn, will prove you wrong." The letter arrived in due course, with the following line after the signature: "P. S. Who is right now, you or I?"

The motion picture producer Samuel Goldwyn said of one of his executives, "We're overpaying him, but he's worth it."

And Yogi Berra said, "No one goes to that restaurant any more; it's too crowded."

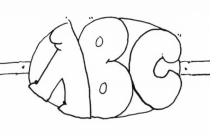

September

1 September

SEPTEMBER

SEPTEMBER should in reason be
    Month Number *Seven*; for the name
In Latin's *seven*. Sorry, we
    And Romans don't count months the same.
(In Roman times, you see, my dear,
The month of *March* began the year.)
                —W.R.E.

BANANANANANANANANANA

I thought I'd win the spelling bee
    And get right to the top,
But I started to spell *banana,*
    And I didn't know when to stop.
            —WILLIAM COLE

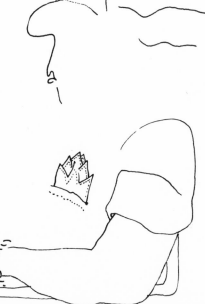

2 September———————————————————

Then Versus Now

Faith Eckler complained that we don't use the language as well as we used to, and gave these examples of the difference:

Then	*Now*
I love thee to the depth and breadth And height my soul can reach.	You turn me on!

—ELIZABETH BARRETT BROWNING

The word must be spoken that bids you depart Though the effort to speak it should shatter my heart.	Get lost!

—GEORGE W. YOUNG

God's in His heaven All's right with the world.	A-OK!

—ROBERT BROWNING

But Faith Eckler was comparing poetry with informal speech. I expect that even a hundred years ago, when the Brownings and George Young were writing, people did not talk as carefully as they wrote.

3 September———————————————————

A, E, I, O, U, and Y

Five words contain the vowels A, E, I, O, and U in order. All five words are adjectives. They are:

- *A*bst*e*m*io*us: Eating and drinking in moderation.
- *A*rs*e*n*io*us: Having to do with a deadly poison.
- *A*rt*e*r*io*us: Having to do with the arteries. Arterial.
- *Ba*ct*e*r*io*us: Having to do with bacteria. Rare for bacterial.
- *Fa*c*e*t*io*us: Humorous; flippant.

Y is an occasional vowel. Add *-ly* to any of the five words, making it an adverb, and you have all six vowels, still in order. Three of the six are concealed below. Which are they?

A, E, I, O, U, and Y
    Congaed down a trail.
Says A to E, ———
    "You're treading on my tail."

To I says O, "The sun is low,
    It's supper time for me."
Says I to that, "You're far too fat;
    Please eat ———"

Says U to Y, "Please hurry, guy,
    You're far behind the train."
Says I, "I fear I'm dying here,
    ——— slain."

            —W.R.E.

4 September———————————————— HASH-HOUSE LANGUAGE

What's Yours, Fella?

The counterman in a hash house may call your order to the cook in terms like these. Do you know what they mean?

1. Draw one!
2. Gimme a shimmy!
3. Side of French!
4. Mickey with a wreath!
5. Mike and Ike!
6. Chocker hole and murk!
7. Arizona!
8. Clean the kitchen, red lead!
9. One on the city!
10. A Coney Island!
11. Garibaldi!
12. BLT, hold the mayo!
13. Whistleberries and hounds, a pair!
14. Bossy in a bowl!
15. Stir two! Wheat!
16. Black and white!
17. Straight Kelly!
18. Eighty-one!
19. Novy on a B!
20. Adam and Eve on a raft!
          —LEONARD R. N. ASHLEY

5 September————————————————

Backward, O Backward

What is *drawer* spelled backward? *Reward.* What is *tar* spelled backward? *Rat.* What is *spar* spelled backward? *Raps.* Words that become other words when the spelling is reversed are *reverse anagrams;* sometimes they are called simply *reversals.* The answer to each of the questions below is a reversal:

- I am dug from the ground. Reverse me, and I am a heavy cotton cloth.
- I am small ponds. Reverse me, and I am a sailboat.
- I am a blow with the open hand. Reverse me, and I am friends.
- I am a heavenly body. Reverse me, and I am rodents.

6 September————————————————

Young Willy, with gobbles and grunts,
Ate his mamma and papa for lunts;
    And when he was through
    He ate himself too,
And didn't say grace even wunts.

              —W.R.E.

A white and a black from Baleen
Took a bath in a washing machine,
    Expecting that they
    Would both come out gray;
But they didn't. They both came out green.*

              —W.R.E.

*But clean.

7 September

Weather or Not

The *Arab News* issued the following bulletin after severe flooding in Jeddah in 1979:

> We regret we are unable to give you the weather. We rely on weather reports from the airport, which is closed because of the weather. Whether we are able to give you the weather tomorrow depends on the weather.

A hurricane is not a hurricane outside the Caribbean Sea. It is a cyclone in the Indian Ocean, and a typhoon in the China Sea.

8 September

Jeremy has just learned these counting rhymes:

I went to a Chinese laundry
To buy a loaf of bread;
They wrapped it up in a tablecloth
And this is what they said:

Rye, chye, chookereye, chookereye,
Choo, choo, ronee, ponee,
Icky, picky, nigh,
Caddy, paddy, vester,
Canlee, poo.
Itty pau, jutty pau,
Chinese stew.

Ra, ra, chuckeree, chuckeree,
Ony, pony,
Ningy, ningy, na,
Addy, caddy, westcy,
Anty, poo.
Chutipan, chutipan,
China, chu.

Then go on to verses like these:

Inty, minty, tippety, fig,
Delia, dilia, dominig;
Eenchi, peenchi, domineechi,
Alm, palm, pus,
Alicka, balicka, boo,
Out goes Y-O-U.

There is nothing to stop you from making up your own counting rhymes.

LETTER-
ADD

9 September

A Row of Rows

Insert the letters *r-o-w* in the place of each set of asterisks below, and you will see what the verse is getting at.

SHIPWRECK

***, ***, *** your boat
    Till the p*** go down;
Fie on him who bor***s sor***:
All must sink and d***n tomorrow;
    All must sink and d***n.

Let no wailing c***d your throat;
    Bar your b*** from f***n;
Bare your breast to Cupid's ar***,
Gnaw the bone and suck the mar***,
    Ere you sink and d***n.

Pluck the blossoms life has g***n,
    Wear them as a c***n;
Many a c*** shall fly from spar***,
Many a lad his *** shall har***
    Ere you sink and d***n.
            —W.R.E.

10 September————————————

Lewd Did I Live

Palindromes are new in English. Until 1820 only one known English sentence read the same way forward or backward: "Lewd did I live & evil I did dwel." It was written by John Taylor, known as the Water Poet, who was born in 1580. Mr. Taylor was a bizarre fellow who advertised himself by performing such stunts as traveling from London to Queensborough in a brown-paper boat. To make his palindrome he had to use & (which is called an ampersand) instead of the word *and;* and he spelled *dwel* with only one *l,* which was perfectly all right in the seventeenth century but would be wrong today.

Nobody came up with another English-language palindrome for nearly two hundred years. Then someone whose name is not known, inspired by the defeat of Napoleon, who was sent into exile at Elba, wrote

Able was I ere I saw Elba.

That opened the floodgates, and new palindromes have been pouring out ever since. Here are a few of the best known:

- Lepers repel.
- Draw pupil's lip upward.
- Egad, a base tone denotes a bad age.
- Name no one man.
- O gnats, tango!
- Step on no pets.
- Sums are not set as a test on Erasmus.

11 September————————————

Manny Who?

Elliott used to be devoted to an old brown ski cap. He refused to take it off. When his mother called him to come and take his bath, Elliott would arrive naked, except for the cap on his head. He did not see why he had to remove it even to wash his hair.

I do not know why I thought of that, because Elliott has put away such childish fancies long since. He prefers now to play brainy games like Knock

Knock. (Of course, not everybody thinks Knock Knock is a very brainy game.) Sometimes he even makes up his own knock knocks.

"Knock knock," he said today.

"Who's there?" I asked.

"Manny."

"Manny who?"

"Manny brave hearts lie asleep in the deep."

He made that one up, but he borrows most of them from joke books. Like these:

ELLIOTT: Knock knock.
MEDORA: Who's there?
ELLIOTT: Noah.
MEDORA: Noah who?
ELLIOTT: Noah body knows the trouble I've seen.

ELLIOTT: Knock knock.
ALEXANDER: Who's there?
ELLIOTT: Huron.
ALEXANDER: Huron who?
ELLIOTT: Huron time for once.

ELLIOTT: Knock knock.
JEREMY: Who's there?
ELLIOTT: Sam.
JEREMY: Sam who?
ELLIOTT: Sam enchanted evening.

LITTLE WILLIES

12 September

Willie saw some dynamite,
Couldn't understand it quite;
Curiosity never pays.
It rained Willie seven days.

———•———

Willie poisoned his father's tea;
Father died in agony.
Mother came, and looked quite vexed:
"Really, Will," she said, "what next?"

Making toast at the fireside
Nurse fell in the grate and died.
But what makes it ten times worse,
All the toast was burnt with Nurse.

———•———

Grandpapa fell down a drain;
Couldn't scramble out again.
Now he's floating down the sewer.
That's one grandpapa the fewer.

—HARRY GRAHAM

Billy fell into the vat,
While his ma was boiling fat.
His father said, "Let's dry our tears—
At least he's clean behind the ears!"

—HUME R. CRAFT

13 September ———————————

Save Me from the Constipation Camp!

"During the war," said a friend of Elliott's, "my father spent two years in a constipation camp." He meant a *concentration* camp.

Another boy called himself a "carnivorous reader." *Carnivorous* means eating only meat; he meant he was *omniverous,* which means eating—or, by extension, taking in—everything available.

A student wrote: "If you get arrested, the police will put your name on the police bladder." A *bladder* is an organ of the body; police put names on a police *blotter.*

A young woman in her first year of college wrote home that she was buying a new dress "for the maternity dance." *Maternity* means mother-hood, and as far as I know there are no maternity dances at college. But there are *fraternity* dances. Fraternities are social clubs for students.

14 September

THE DINERS IN THE KITCHEN

Our dog Fred
Et the bread

Our dog Dash
Et the hash

Our dog Pete
Et the meat

Our dog Davy
Et the gravy

Our dog Toffy
Et the coffee

And—the worst
From the first—

Our dog Fido
Et the pie-dough.
—JAMES WHITCOMB RILEY

15 September

Hooligan, Hoodlum

An Irish family named Hooligan, who lived in London at the end of the nineteenth century, were such rough characters that law-abiding citizens ran when they saw a Hooligan coming. The word came to mean "roughneck," and quickly entered many other languages. Even the Russians call people they do not like "hooligans."

———•———

A rough fellow named Muldoon was leader of a street gang that terrorized the San Francisco waterfront in the 1870s. The newspapers were said to be so terrified of him that they did not dare print his name right. They spelled it backward, and changed the *n* to an *h*. *Muldoon* became *hoodlum*. Like *hooligan*, *hoodlum* is now a common word for a street tough.

16 September——————————— NONSENSE

WAY DOWN SOUTH WHERE BANANAS GROW

Way down South where bananas grow
A grasshopper stepped on an elephant's toe.
The elephant said, with tears in his eyes,
"Pick on somebody your own size."

SUCH A SHOCK

It's such a shock, I almost screech,
When I find a worm inside my peach!
But then, what *really* makes me blue
Is to find a worm who's bit in two!
—WILLIAM COLE

17 September——————————— STORY

How the King Found His Crown: III *

This is the last part of Medora's story about the king.

Chapter III: The king found his crown

The watere served the soup.
What is the soup today?
Chowder sir sead the watere
Chowder dosent have a lump in it
let me see sir sed the wadere
The king put his spoon in the soup. It clanged.
Soup doesn't clang. sed the king theres something in her
He pooct around in his soup. heres my crown!! Wut is my crown doing
in the soup?
the king was very happy. for a few days his crown smelled of chowder
but he dident minde.

The Aend

—MEDORA

*Continued from 7 August.

18 September————————————————————

WHO'S JOANNA?

Today is Joanna's birthday, so we sang this song for her:

Who's Joanna? Who is she?—
Born in Anno Domini . . .
Was it 1970?
No—nor 1, nor 2, nor 3,
Nor 4. Joanna's been alive
Just since 1-9-7-5.

    Then I went back to my room and wrote this verse, which has nothing to do with Joanna at all:

SIPPING CIDER ON THE ZUYDER ZEE

She wallowed in the Zuyder Zee,
The breeze had ceased to spank;
The crew of her was him and me,
A Dutchman and a Yank.

Inside her there was cider, there was cider in the sea,
And cider on the starboard side, the larboard side, the lee,
And much of such inside the Dutch, and much of such in me.

From starboard spake the Dutchman, and fully merrily spake he:
"The starboard is the steer-board side, so steer me two or three;
And when we've sipped the cider, we will sip the cider sea."

From larboard then the Yankee spake, the Yankee being me,
"The larboard is the loading side, so load in two or three.
We'll sip up all the cider, see, and then the Zuyder Zee."

—W.R.E.

19 September————————————————————

Unlikely Words

How many words end in -dous? Five: *hazardous, horrendous, stupendous, pudendous,* and *tremendous.* Hazardous means risky; horrendous means hideous; stupendous means marvelous; pudendous means related to the sexual organs; tremendous means enormous.

Are there any words besides *hungry* and *angry* that end in *-gry*? Yes, two: *aggry*, a kind of ancient glass bead found on the Gold Coast of West Africa; and *puggry*, a light scarf wound around the hat or helmet in India for protection from the sun.

20 September ————————————

The Irish Don't Mind

"What's an Irish spoon?" asked Alexander.
   "A shovel," said Medora.
   "What's an Irish buggy?" asked Elliott.
   "A wheelbarrow," said Taylor.
   "What's Irish confetti?" asked Joanna.
   "Bricks," said Jeremy.
   "What's an Irish clubhouse?" asked Alexander.
   "A police station," said Taylor.
   "What's an Irish nightingale?" asked Joanna.
   "A bullfrog," said Medora.

WHEN A NIRRUP IS A PRONKUS

Don't say there isn't any rhyme for *stirrup*.
Some English farmers call their donkeys *nirrup*—
Or *mokus, fussock, cuddy, dicky, pronkus!*
(To make this rhyme, I'll call my donkey *donkus*.)
—W.R.E.

21 September ————————————

ELLIOTT: Why is a balloon like a beggar?
ALEXANDER: Because it has no visible means of support.

ELLIOTT: Why does a music teacher have to be a good teacher?
ALEXANDER: Because she's a sound instructor.

ELLIOTT: Why is a nobleman like a book?
ALEXANDER: Because he has a title.

ELLIOTT: What bird is present at every meal?
ALEXANDER: The swallow.

ALEXANDER: What is it about coffee that keeps you awake?
ELLIOTT: The high price.

ELLIOTT: Where does Monday come before Sunday?
ALEXANDER: In the dictionary.

ALEXANDER: What did the duck say when it laid a square egg?
ELLIOTT: Ouch!

DIALECT **22 September**

Framed in a First-story Winder

Some people in London speak a dialect called Cockney, which drops the sound of *h* at the beginning of a word. This is Alexander's favorite verse in Cockney:

Framed in a first-story winder of a burnin' buildin'
Appeared: A Yuman Ead!
Jump into this net, wot we are 'oldin'
And yule be quite orl right!

But 'ee wouldn't jump. . . .

And the flames grew Igher and Igher and Igher.
(Phew!)

Framed in a second-story winder of a burnin' buildin'
Appeared: A Yuman Ead!
Jump into this net, wot we are 'oldin'
And yule be quite orl right!

But 'ee wouldn't jump. . . .

And the flames grew Igher and Igher and Igher
(Strewth!)

Framed in a third-story winder of a burnin' buildin'
Appeared: A Yuman Ead!
Jump into this net, wot we are 'oldin'
And yule be quite orl right!
Honest!

And 'ee jumped. . . .
And 'ee broke 'is bloomin' neck!

23 September

Bunk, Book

When you say, "That's the bunk!" you are shortening the name of the county of Buncombe, North Carolina. Felix Walker, who was congressman for Buncombe County in 1819, used to make pointless speeches. He would explain that he was speaking for the benefit of the voters in Buncombe, who would read what he had said in the *Congressional Record*. So meaningless talk came to be called *buncombe,* which, as the years passed, was shortened to *bunk.*

Where does the word *book* come from? From the Old English word for a beech tree—*bōc.* Priests used to scratch their sermons on the inner bark of beech trees. (The word *write* first meant to scratch!)

24 September

THE END-OF-SUMMER TENNIS SHOES BLUES

The tread is gone
from both the soles,
And both the toes
are full of holes.

But that is not
the worst of it—
My tennis shoes
no longer fit!

Sing the end-of-summer blues,
Good-bye, my old tennis shoes.
—JUDITH UNTER

25 September

These spoonerisms were mistakes of radio and television announcers:

- Why not try Cretty Booper's poo seep—I mean see poop—I mean soo peep?
- Mr. Jones will now play a slote flulo.

- We proudly present the newted nose analyst. . . .
- Come to Tom's restaurant for chickasee fricken.
- You will know the president has arrived when you hear a twenty-one-sun galoot.
- Several of the women here tonight are wearing gownless evening straps.

LOGIC 26 September

Asparagus Logic

"I'm so glad I don't like asparagus," said Medora.
"Why not?" asked Jeremy.
"Because if I did, I should have to eat it, and I can't stand it."
I said, "Medora, did you make that up?"
"No," said Medora. "Our teacher said that Lewis Carroll made it up."

Elliott saw this sign in the window of a music shop:
GONE CHOPIN, BACH IN A MINUET.

Alexander tells me the longest one-syllable word in English is *strengths*. It has nine letters, and only one vowel.

NONSENSE 27 September

Why Don't It Rain on You?

Alexander, Elliott, Jeremy, Medora, Joanna, and Taylor stood in front of me in a row.

"We've come to serenade you, Pop," said Elliott.
This is the song they sang:

Oh, the train pulled in the station.
The bell was ringing wet.
The track ran by the depot,
And I think it's running yet.

'Twas midnight on the ocean,
Not a streetcar was in sight.
The sun and moon were shining,
And it rained all day that night.

'Twas a summer day in winter,
    And the snow was raining fast
As a barefoot boy with shoes on
    Stood sitting in the grass.

Oh, I jumped into the river
    Just because it had a bed.
I took a sheet of water
    For to cover up my head.

Oh, the rain makes all things beautiful,
    The flowers and grasses, too.
If the rain makes all things beautiful,
    Why don't it rain on you?

28 September

Split-level Words

Some words have split personalities, that is they mean different things at different times. Take these, for example:

- A *bluff* is a high cliff. To *bluff* is to pretend strength you don't have.
- A *bust* is a piece of sculpture representing the head and upper part of the body. To *bust* is to break.
- To *spell* is to write the letters that make up a word. It is also to do someone's job so he can rest.
- One's *rank* is one's position or grade in a group. ("His rank was sergeant-major.") As an adjective, *rank* is having a bad smell, or indecent, or growing profusely.
- A *hamper* is a large basket. To *hamper* is to hinder.
- A *bolt* is a bar or rod that slides into a socket. To *bolt* is to run away.
- A *post* is an upright stake. To *post* is to bob up and down in rhythm on a horse, or to send something by mail, or to make entries in a ledger.

29 September————————————————

The moon told an old man in Axing,
"My job is becoming too taxing.
　　I don't mind the heights,
　　Or the working at nights,
But I'm sick of the waning and waxing."
　　　　　　　　　—W.R.E.

My TV came down with a chill.
As soon as I saw it was ill
　　I wrapped up its channels
　　In warm winter flannels
And gave its antenna a pill.
　　　　　　　—W.R.E.

There once was a fish in a brook
Who dreamed he had swallowed a hook.
　　He found when he woke
　　The dream was no joke—
He was already starting to cook.
　　　　　　　—W.R.E.

30 September————————————————

IF I SHOULD DIE
　　If I should die tonight
And you should come to my cold corpse and say,
Weeping and heartsick o'er my lifeless clay—
　　If I should die tonight,
And you should come in deepest grief and woe—
And say: "Here's that ten dollars that I owe,"
　　I might arise in my large white cravat
　　And say, "What's that?"

　　If I should die tonight
And you should come to my cold corpse and kneel,
Clasping my bier to show the grief you feel,
　　I say, if I should die tonight
And you should come to me, and there and then
Just even hint 'bout payin' me that ten,
　　I might arise the while,
　　But I'd drop dead again.
　　　　　　　—BEN KING

October

1 October

OCTOBER

It's O and C and T and O and B and E and R:
Come daddy dear it's time to go, the kids
    are in the car;
The jack o'lantern twinkles, and the cats
    are out of tune;
We'll watch the witches streaming past the
    sickle of the moon.

        —W.R.E.

OCTOBER

O hushed October morning mild,
    Thy leaves have ripened to the fall;
Tomorrow's wind, if it be wild,
    Should waste them all.
    The crows above the forest call;
Tomorrow they may form and go.
    O hushed October morning mild,
Begin the hours of this day slow.
    Make the day seem to us less brief.
Hearts not averse to being beguiled
    Beguile us in the way you know.
Release one leaf at break of day;
    At noon release another leaf;
One from our trees, one far away.
    Retard the sun with gentle mist;
    Enchant the land with amethyst.
Slow, slow!
For the grapes' sake, if they were all,
    Whose leaves are already burnt with frost,
Whose clustered fruit must else be lost—
    For the grapes' sake along the wall.

        —ROBERT FROST

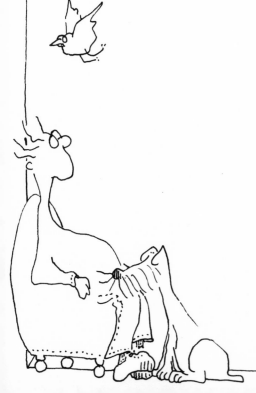

2 October

- Polygon: A dead parrot
- Catalyst: (1) Angora (2) Siamese (3) Persian
- Doggerel: Sister of Dogboy
- Incongruous: Where laws are made
- Toboggan: To haggle
- Tuscaloosa: Elephant disease

—DAVID GOLDBERG

3 October

CAN WE WRITE THIS WRONG?
We're on speaking terms with the phrase "on the double,"
But say "on the single," and, boy, you're in trouble.

Take "nevertheless"—we hear it galore,
Yet nary a murmur of "neverthemore."

Note this: "in the long run"—unless it's a race;
Why not "in the long walk" to slacken the pace?

Of course "notwithstanding," but no, it's unfitting
Wherever you're standing to say "notwithsitting."

If facts are "forthcoming," we'd feel better knowing
That sooner or later they will be "forthgoing."

—A.S. FLAUMENHAFT

4 October

JEREMY: Three men fell into the water, but only two got their hair wet.
MEDORA: Why?
JEREMY: One man was bald.

ELLIOTT: What's your cat's name?
MEDORA: Ben Hur.
ELLIOTT: Why did you give it such an odd name?
MEDORA: Well, we used to call it just Ben. But then it had kittens.

ELLIOTT: What did the envelope say to the stamp?
JEREMY: You may be square, but you sure do send me!

ELLIOTT: Why is the air so much cleaner in New York City?
JEREMY: Because they have skyscrapers.

5 October————————————————— ANIMALS

ANIMAL SOUNDS

The cry of a cat's a meow,
　　And an oink is the meow of a hog;
And a moo is the oink of a cow,
　　And a bark is the moo of a dog;

And a neigh is the bark of a horse,
　　And a trumpet's an elephant's neigh;
And the trumpets of lions are roars,
　　And the roar of a donkey's a bray.

And the bray of a duck is a quack,
　　And the quack of a snake is a hiss;
And if that doesn't take you aback,
　　You may be confounded by this:

The hiss of a sheep is a baa,
　　And a hyena's baa is a laugh;
And the laugh of a babe is a waah,
　　And the waah of a . . . say a . . . giraffe
　　Is so small
　　　　It is nothing
　　　　　　Nothing at all.
　　　　　　—W.R.E.

6 October

Sweet William's Stinky Billy, and Canary Is a Dog

You will see in many gardens a beautiful plant called Sweet William, with dense clusters of flowers of many colors. It is named after an Englishman, William, Duke of Cumberland, whose army whipped the Scots in the Battle of Culloden (1746). But the Scots call him Butcher Cumberland—and the flower, "stinky Billy."

———•———

A canary is a greenish-yellow songbird that originated in the Canary Islands, in the Atlantic Ocean off the northwestern corner of Africa. But the name of the island—and so of the birds—is from Latin *canes,* "dog," because of the wild dogs that the first settlers found there.

7 October

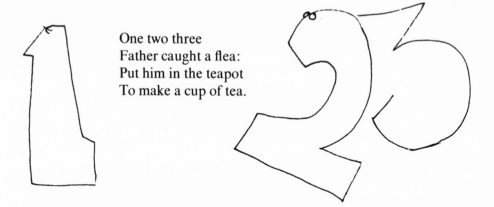

One two three
Father caught a flea:
Put him in the teapot
To make a cup of tea.

There was a young lady residing at Prague
Whose ideas were really most wonderfully vague.
When anyone said to her: "What a fine day!"
"Roast chicken is nice," she would dreamily say,
"And a mushroom on toast is the very best thing
To make a canary or hummingbird sing."
The people of Prague thought this conduct so strange,
They quickly decided she needed a change,
So packed her with care in a box with some hay,
And paid her expenses as far as Bombay.

8 October ──────────────────────────────

Here are more palindromes (by now you know they're passages that read the same forward or backward):

- Doc, note, I dissent. A fast never prevents a fatness. I diet on cod.
  —PENELOPE GILLIATT

- I moan, Naomi.
- Norma is as selfless as I am, Ron.
- Never odd or even.

This is a make-believe interview with Professor R. Osseforp (backward for professor), holder of the Emor D. Nilap (backward for palindrome) Chair in Palindromology at Harvard:

"And what about your new novel, could you tell me the title?"

"Dennis Sinned."

"Intriguing. What is the plot?"

"Dennis and Edna sinned."

"I see. Is there more to it than that?"

"Dennis Krats and Edna Stark sinned."

"Now it all becomes clear. Tell me, with all this concern about ecology, what kind of car are you driving nowadays?"

"A Toyota."

"Naturally, and how about your colleague, Professor Nustad?"

"Nustad? A Datsun."

—SOLOMON W. GOLOMB

(Ralph G. Beaman added these two lines:)

"And his wife May?"

"Aha! May? A Yamaha!"

9 October

Two Young Men

Salisbury, in England, used to be pronounced Sārum; I have no idea why. Hampshire is abbreviated Hants; I don't know why that is, either. Anyway, with those two clues, you should be able to make sense of the following limerick:

THE YOUNG CURATE OF SALISBURY

There was a young curate of Salisbury,
Whose manners were quite halisbury-scalisbury.
    He ran around Hampshire
    Without any pampshire,
Till the vicar compelled him to walisbury.

To understand the next verse, you need to know that the English pronounce the name Cholmondeley "Chumley," and the name Colquhoun "Coon."

A YOUNG MAN CALLED CHOLMONDELEY COLQUHOUN

A young man called Cholmondeley Colquhoun
Kept as a pet a babolquhoun.
    His mother said, "Cholmondeley,
    Do you think it quite colmendeley
To feed your babolquhoun with a spquhoun?"

          —A.D. HOPE

10 October

"The little moron was waiting for a 'phone call," said Medora, "and couldn't wait any longer; so he took the receiver off the hook and left a note."

"The little moron lost his watch on top of a hill," said Elliott, "but he wouldn't go back for it. He knew it would run down."

"The little moron wrote letters to his girl very slowly," said Jeremy. "He said she couldn't read very fast."

"The little moron went to a show," said Alexander, "and was asked whether he wanted to sit in the balcony or on the main floor. He said, 'What's playing upstairs?' "

The little moron and a friend were watching the eleven o'clock news on television. They saw a man standing on the ledge of an office building, ready to jump.

"I'll bet you a dollar he doesn't jump," said the little moron.

"I'll bet you a dollar he does," said his friend.

The man jumped. "Here's your dollar," said the little moron.

"Oh, I shouldn't take it," said his friend. "I saw him on the six-thirty news, and I knew he jumped."

"I saw him on the six-thirty news too," said the little moron. "But I didn't think he would be silly enough to jump twice."

11 October————————————————

HOW MUCH DID PHILADELPHIA PA?

How much did Philadelphia Pa?
    Whose grass did K. C. Mo?
How many eggs could New Orleans La?
    How much does Cleveland O?

When Hartford and New Haven Conn
    What sucker do they soak?
Could Noah build a Little Rock Ark
    If he had not Guthrie Ok?

We call Minneapolis Minn,
    Why not Annapolis Ann?
If you can't tell the reason why
    I'll bet Topeka Kan.

But now we speak of ladies, what
    A Butte Montana is!
If I could borrow Memphis Tenn
    I'd treat that Jackson Miss.

Would Denver Colo cop because
    Ottumwa Ia dore?
Ah, though my Portland Me doth love,
    I threw my Portland Ore.

12 October—

HAPPY BIRTHDAY, ALEXANDER!

Christopher Columb,
An apple tree he clumb.
An apple dropped upon his head;
Christopher Columb, he said,
   "This gives me a
   Good idea:
   I'll invent
   A continent
So that Alexander may
Be born there on Columbus Day."

—W.R.E.

(The apple really dropped on Sir Isaac Newton's head. It gave him a new idea about the laws of physics. But if it worked for Newton, who can say it would not have worked for Columbus?)

13 October—

"My Fellow Convicts . . ."

Governor Al Smith of New York was giving a talk to the inmates of Sing Sing Prison. "My fellow citizens . . ." he began, but then he recalled that convicts are no longer citizens. So he corrected himself: "My fellow convicts. . . ." But that wasn't right either, so he changed to, "Well, anyhow, I'm glad to see so many of you here."

Here are a few such slips from newspapers:

- We have the same eggs for sale that we had last winter. Come and see us.
- We Do Not Tear Your Clothes with Machinery. We Do It Carefully by Hand.
- Ski conditions ideal; only ten injured
- From a TV program listing:
  9:00 Geo. Gobel Show
  9:15 Geo. Gobel Shot
- Mrs. Carl Treaster slipped on the ice and hurt her somewhat.
- Miss Rogers was winking for the third time when the lifeguard seized her and dragged her ashore.

From a column of advice to husbands and wives:

· When she washes dishes, he should wash dishes with her, and when she mops up the floor, he should mop up the floor with her.

14 October————————————————

O U Q-T!

When translating ABC language into everyday English, it is useful to bear in mind that the sounds of letters and numerals need not be *exactly* the same as the sounds of the syllables and words they stand for. O U Q-T is exactly the sound of "Oh, you cutie," but R U C-P is not exactly the sound of "Are you sleepy," nor is S S exactly the sound of "This is." They are just close enough to help you guess what is meant. A hyphen between two or more letters means that they make one word.

ALEXANDER (to Medora, who has just done a handstand):   I N-V U.

MEDORA (to Jeremy, who is yawning):   R U C-P?
JEREMY: S I M.
MEDORA: I M C-P 2.

ELLIOTT (in a flower garden):   O C D B!
MEDORA: D B S A B-Z B.
ELLIOTT: O S! D B S 2 B-Z!

JEREMY (presenting a flower to Medora):   S S A P-N-E 4 U.

ALEXANDER (to Jeremy, who has hit his head against a fence post):   R U O-K?
JEREMY: S, I M O-K, N Q.

JEREMY (giving Medora a kiss on the cheek):   O U Q-T. U R A B-U-T.

MEDORA (to Elliott, who has found a hen's nest with eggs in it):   C, D N S X!
ELLIOTT: S, I C. D N S 5 X.

ALEXANDER (at the seashore):   I C D C-L. D C-L S N D C.
JEREMY (not at the seashore):   I C D D-R. D D-R S N D I-V.

15 October ———————————————

The Everlasting Light Bulb

Many things may be getting better in the world, but electric light bulbs do not seem to be among them. In 1979 most light bulbs could be used for 750 hours before they burned out. But in 1933 they could be burned for 1,000 hours. And the last I heard, a light bulb made by the Shelby Electric Company, which was installed in the Fire Department at Livermore, California, in 1901, was still doing fine after having been used almost continuously for eighty years.

16 October ———————————————

As I was going out one day
My head fell off and rolled away.
But when I saw that it was gone,
I picked it up and put it on.

And when I got into the street
A fellow cried: "Look at your feet!"
I looked at them and sadly said:
"I've left them both asleep in bed."

I dreamed a dream next Tuesday week
    Beneath the apple trees;
I thought my eyes were big pork pies,
    And my nose was Stilton cheese.
The clock struck twenty minutes to six
    As a frog jumped on my knee;
I asked him to lend me a quarter,
    But he borrowed a dollar from me.

17 October ———————————————

Each of the missing words in the two verses below has the same letters, differently arranged. See if you can guess the words.

The _ _ _ _ _ truth I must relate:
The queen won't wear her _ _ _ _ _ of state.
It _ _ _ _ _ her when the Royal Guard

Mistake her for a playing card.
    (One of the anagram words is *robes.*)

—•—

"_ _ _ _, say where _ _ _ _ cheese comes from,
   comes from?"
"Cow's milk; I milk them by the sea, the sea."

"And what is _ _ _ _ _ _ _ _ from, old chum, old chum?"
"Bee's milk; but they aren't milked by me,
      by me."
      (One of the anagram words is *Edam,* a kind of cheese.)
                                                    —W.R.E.

18 October—————————————————

AUTUMN

There is wind where the rose was;
Cold rain where sweet grass was;
      And clouds like sheep
      Stream o'er the steep
Grey skies where the lark was.

Nought gold where your hair was;
Nought warm where your hand was;
      But phantom, forlorn,
      Beneath the thorn,
Your ghost where your face was.

Sad winds where your voice was;
Tears, tears where my heart was;
      And ever with me,
      Child, ever with me,
Silence where hope was.
                        —WALTER DE LA MARE

19 October—————————————————

There's a beautiful girl in the skies
Of an astronomical size.
      I gaze through my 'scope
      Each night in the hope
Of seeing the stars in her eyes.
                        —W.R.E.

An amoeba inside my inside
Put on so much weight that it cried—
      Till another one said,
      "Don't worry your head;
You are only about to divide."
                        —W.R.E.

20 October

Calm, Dunce

Calm, in Greek, means "burning heat." During the burning heat of midday, sensible Athenians took a nap; so the meaning of *calm* gradually changed from heat to restfulness.

———•———

Dunce was the name of a very wise man. Duns Scotus, a Scot, was a leading philosopher of the Middle Ages. But his followers, the Dunsians, were so stubborn in insisting on his views that they came to be thought of as idiots. Dunces.

21 October

TAME ANIMALS I HAVE KNOWN
A thick-fleeced lamb came trotting by:
"Pray whither now, my lamb," quoth I.
"To have," said he with ne'er a stop
"My wool clipped at the baa baa shop."

I asked the cat: "Pray tell me why
You love to sing?" She blinked her eye.
"My purr-puss, sir, as you can see,
Is to amuse myself," said she.
—NIXON WATERMAN

22 October

Alexander Says It Right

When I asked Alexander today why he was laughing so hard, he showed me these mixed-up sayings:

- The use of drugs is on the upcrease.
- The circumstances are on the other foot.
- I don't pull any bones about it.
- You're talking around the bush.
- You are out of your rocker.
- You set my hair on edge.
- He will lend an ear to anyone who wants to listen.

—JAMES D. WHITE

23 October ——————————

I Saw a Peacock with a Fiery Tail

Punctuate this verse (comma, semicolon, or period) so that it makes sense. Begin thus: I saw a peacock; with a fiery tail I saw a blazing comet; and so on. (When this poem was written, a long time ago, people turned their sentences around—"inverted" them, that is—more often than they do now. I never heard of their saying anything so unlikely as, say, "drop down hail I saw a cloud;" but after all, that is just a turn-around of "I saw a cloud drop down hail.")

I saw a peacock with a fiery tail
I saw a blazing comet drop down hail
I saw a cloud wrapped with ivy round
I saw an oak creep on along the ground
I saw a pismire swallow up a whale
I saw the sea brimful of ale
I saw a Venice glass full fathom deep
I saw a well full of men's tears that weep
I saw red eyes all of a flaming fire
I saw a house bigger than the moon and higher
I saw the sun at twelve o'clock at night
I saw the man that saw this wondrous sight.

24 October ——————————

A Fable by Aesop

On 16 March Alexander and Jeremy located hidden animals in sentences by finding successive letters in the sentence that made the name of an animal. (Just to remind you, the hidden word in the sentence "If Mr. Jones should stop, ignore him," is *pig,* from sto*p ig*nore.) Use the same system now to find a hidden word in each of the four lines below: first, an animal; second, a two-letter preposition; third, another animal; fourth, what we wear. Taken in order, the words will give you the title of a fable by Aesop.

1. The G.I. went AWOL for four days.
2. I never saw you looking more beautiful, dear.
3. I don't believe you heard the wail of a banshee;
   pshaw, there is no such thing as a banshee.
4. Casey's at bat; a terrific lot hinges on whether
   he makes a hit.

25 October

Elliott's Favorite Counting-out Rhymes

Engine, engine, number nine,
Running on Chicago line;
When she's polished, she will shine.
Engine, engine, number nine.
O-U-T spells out goes he,
Into the middle of the dark blue sea.

Paddy on the railway
Picking up the stones;
Along came an engine
And broke Paddy's bones.
Oh, said Paddy,
That's not fair.
Pooh, said the engine driver,
I don't care.
O-U-T goes he.

Each, peach, pear, plum,
Out goes Tom Thumb;
Tom Thumb won't do,
Out goes Betty Blue;
Betty Blue won't go,
So O-U-T goes you.

26 October

Elliott asked Medora to write down any three-digit number without letting
him know what it was. Then he asked her to repeat it to make a six-digit
number. (If she had chosen 216, she would now have 216,216; if she had
chosen 523, she would have 523,523, and so on.) Then he frowned hard for a
moment, and said, "I don't know what your number is, but it can be divided
evenly by seven."

He was right. And he would have been right if he had said it could be
divided evenly by 11, or 13. The reason is that when three digits are repeated to make six digits, the six-digit number is always exactly 1,001 times
the original three-digit number. And 1,001 is the product of three prime
numbers: $7 \times 11 \times 13 = 1,001$. So any number that is multiplied by 1,001
must be divisible by 7, 11, or 13.

Buzz and bizz and bizz and buzz,
Bee and mee, that's how it was.
Bizz and buzz and buzz and bizz,
Bee and mee, that's how it izz.
No more bizz, buzz, bee or mee;
That's the way that it will bee.
—W.R.E.

————•————

If all the seas were one sea,
What a *great* sea that would be!
And if all the trees were one tree,
What a *great* tree that would be!
And if all the axes were one axe,
What a *great* axe that would be!
And if all the men were one man,
What a *great* man he would be!
And if the *great* man took the *great* axe,
And cut down the *great* tree,
And let it fall into the *great* sea,
What a splish-splash *that* would be!

MEDORA: What is a parriger?
JEREMY: A cross between a parrot and a tiger.
MEDORA: Can it talk?
JEREMY: Not much. But when it does—run!

JEREMY: How can I get hens to lay boiled eggs?
MEDORA: Feed them boiling water.

MEDORA: Every day my dog and I go for a tramp in the woods.
JEREMY: Sounds like fun.
MEDORA: Yes, but the tramp's getting pretty cranky about it.

MEDORA: Did you know insects can cry?
JEREMY: Sure. Haven't you ever seen a mothball?

29 October

The Clever Carver

Here is one of the stories Mala Powers tells:

> There was a rich man who, long ago, lived in China.
> One day, he called two carvers to his home.
> "Carve a mouse for me," he said, "and I will give a bag of gold for the best mouse."
> A few days later, the two men returned with their carvings.
> One was a lovely wooden mouse. The second was of a flaky material and didn't look much like a mouse.
> When the cat came in, it pounced on the flaky, funny-looking carving.
> "Your carving doesn't even look like a mouse," said the rich man. "Why did my cat pounce on it?"
> "I carved my mouse from dried fish," replied the second carver.
> "Well," laughed the rich man, "here are *two* bags of gold. One for the carver who made the lifelike mouse. The other for the second carver for being so clever. I will keep the wooden mouse. My cat can have the other one."

MORE RI-DICULOUS RIDDLES

30 October

JEREMY: What is a secret?
ALEXANDER: Something you tell only one person at a time.

MEDORA: When I grow up I am not going to think about boys.
ELLIOTT: Why not?
MEDORA: I am going to think about men.

ELLIOTT: What is adolescence?
JEREMY: When a girl begins to powder and a boy begins to puff.

ELLIOTT: What is the best way to discipline boys?
MEDORA: Start at the bottom.

ELLIOTT: Where do you find horse sense?
JEREMY: In a stable mind.

WITCHES' WORK SONG

Two spoons of sherry
Three oz. of yeast,
Half a pound of unicorn,
And God bless the feast.
Shake them in the collander,
Bang them to a chop,
Simmer slightly, snip up nicely,
Jump, skip, hop.
Knit one, knot one, purl two together,
Pip one and pop one and pluck the secret feather.
Baste in mod. oven.
God bless our coven.
Tra-la-la!
Three toads in a jar.
Te-he-he!
Put in the frog's knee.
Peep out of the lace curtain.
There goes the Toplady girl, she's up to no good,
    that's certain.
Oh, what a lovely baby!
How nice it would go with gravy.
Pinch the salt,
Turn the malt
With a hey-nonny-nonny and I don't mean maybe.

—T. H. WHITE

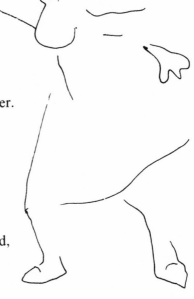

How does a witch know when it is midnight on Halloween?
She looks at her witch watch.

November

1 November

What good is to be said of November? Well, there is Thanksgiving, and we know that Christmas is on the way. Otherwise I agree with the writer of this verse, that it's not much of a month.

NO!

No sun—no moon!
No morn—no noon—
No dawn—no dusk—no proper time of day—
No sky—no earthly view—
No distance looking blue—
No road—no street—no "t'other side the way"—
No top to any steeple—
No recognitions of familiar people—
No courtesies for showing 'em—
No knowing 'em!
No traveling at all—no locomotion—
No inkling of the way—no notion—
"No go" by land or ocean—
No mail—no post—
No news from any foreign coast—
No park—no ring—no afternoon gentility—
No company—no nobility—
No warmth, no cheerfulness, no healthful ease,
No comfortable feel in any member—
No shade, no shine, no butterflies, no bees,
No fruits, no flowers, no leaves, no birds.
November!

—THOMAS HOOD

2 November—————————

Daffy Definitions

Sometimes a word sounds as if it means something quite different from its real definition. *Largess,* for instance, sounds like "large S," but really means "giving generously." *Mandate* sounds as if it means "a male escort," but really means "an authoritative command." What words sound as if they fit the definitions below?

1. Wedding day
2. Judge's robe
3. Faint noise (or wild movement)
4. Ready hat
5. Ex-spouse
6. Fake diamond

3 November—————————

We're all in the dumps,
For diamonds are trumps,
  The kittens are gone to St. Paul's.
The babies are bit,
The moon's in a fit,
  And the houses are built without walls.

———•———

The rain it raineth on the just
  And also on the unjust fella.
But chiefly on the just, because
  The unjust steals the just's umbrella.
    —BARON CHARLES BOWEN

4 November—————————

Ukulele, Boulevard

In the nineteenth century a British officer named Purvis (some say the spelling was Putvis) retired to Hawaii. Because of his miniature size and lively ways, the natives called him Little Flea. Little Flea became expert on a stringed instrument similar to the banjo, brought to the islands by Portuguese workmen; it was played with the fingers in a fashion that reminded the natives of a flea hopping. So they gave the musical instrument the same name they had applied to the man who played it so well. Little Flea it still is, and Little Flea in Hawaiian is . . . ukulele.

A *boulevard* is an important street or promenade, a place to walk. It used to mean just the opposite. It was French for "bulwark," "rampart," and referred to the walls built around a city to protect it. When the custom of besieging cities faded away, and the walls were no longer needed for defense, the city fathers turned the boulevards into elevated promenades.

NONSENSE

5 November

THE ERASER POEM

The eraser poem.
The eraser poem
The eraser poe
The eraser po
The eraser p
The eraser
The erase
The eras
The era
The er
The e
The
Th
T
-

—LOUIS PHILLIPS

**WORD
GAME**

6 November

What Does It Mean?

In this game, the person asked to tell what a word means does not define the word; he or she gives an answer that *shows* the meaning.

MEDORA: Do you know what *procrastination* is?
ALEXANDER: I've been meaning to look it up.

JOANNA: Do you know what *conciseness* is?
TAYLOR: Yes.

ELLIOTT: Do you know what *irritability* is?
JEREMY: Stop bothering me with silly questions.

—JANE BARLISS

7 November

MEDORA: Elliott, why are you swimming with your socks on?
ELLIOTT: The water is cold this time of year.

JOANNA: I learned to write in school today.
MEDORA: What did you write?
JOANNA: I don't know. I haven't learned to read yet.

ELLIOTT: I hear the police are looking for a man with one eye called Murphy.
JEREMY: Oh—what is his other eye called?

MEDORA: Those bananas you brought me yesterday were green and terribly hard to peel.
JEREMY: What do you expect—zippers?

8 November

An ancient anteater named Chung
Has flickers that nest on his tongue.
    They perch on his snout,
    And dart in and out,
And steal his best ants for their young.
        —W.R.E.

Medora asked me what the verse below means. What could I say? The whole point is that it means nothing.

HE: Fiddle dee carra wee loop?
SHE: Crahmer om ib corser soop.
HE: Coggle con see?
SHE: Ara lig dee.
HE: Hoggle O soggle poop poop!
        —W.R.E.

9 November

Malo Malo, Ma Ma

The four Latin words *Malo malo malo malo* can be translated loosely into English as

> I'd rather be
> In an apple tree
> Than a bad man
> In adversity.

And if you say "Ma ma ma ma ma" in the Shan language of Burma, with a different inflection on each "ma," the words mean, "Help the horse; a mad dog is coming."

10 November

It was a dark and stormy night. The robbers were sitting about a fire. "Tell us a story," said one robber to another. So the second robber began, "It was a dark and stormy night. The robbers were sitting around a fire. 'Tell us a story,' said one robber to another. So the second robber began . . . .'"

> I am a funny fellow,
>   And what do you think I do?
> I dress myself in yellow,
>   And drink a drink or two,
> And as I drink I bellow
>   These lovely lines for you:
> "I am a funny fellow. . ."
>   —W.R.E.

> I saw a parrot yesternight,
>   A-sitting in a tree,
> And when he saw I saw him,
>   The parrot said to me,
> "I saw a parrot yesternight,
>   A-sitting in a tree . . ."
>   —W.R.E.

You can go on and on this way.

11 November

VOTER'S COMPLAINT

I voted for the _ _ _ _ _ of candidates
Who, if elected, seemed _ _ _ _ _ _ apt to _ _ _ _ _ _.
Now from the _ _ _ _ _ _ I hear there emanates
The old _ _ _ _ _ story of a double deal.

    (One of the anagram words is *steal.*)

———•———

He _ _ _ _ _ for gold,
As I for ale;
I've _ _ _ _ _ of this;
Of that has he.
For me a kiss
_ _ _ _ _ Holy Grail;
He'd beat his wife
To _ _ _ _ _ a fee.
Yet, _ _ _ _ _ ! I wis
(And I'd _ _ _ _ _ bail)
He'd pay fourfold
To be like me.

    (One of the anagram words is *post.*)

        —W.R.E.

12 November

Medora's Counting-out Rhymes

These are Medora's favorite counting-out rhymes to see who will be "it" in a game.

Eeny, meeny, miney, mo,
Catch a monkey by the toe,
If he hollers, let him go.
Eeny, meeny, miney, mo.

———•———

Inky, pinky, ponky,
My daddy bought a donkey,
The donkey died,
Daddy cried,
Inky, pinky, ponky.

———•———

Red, white, and blue,
The cat's got the flu,
The baby has the whooping cough
And out goes you.

———•———

Round and round the butter dish
One, two, three,
If you like a nice girl,
Please pick me.

13 November——————————————

Kickle Snifters

Alexander and Elliott and Medora and Jeremy took turns reading a book. The book was *Kickle Snifters,* by Alvin Schwartz; it described creatures that maybe don't really exist.

"I like the rubberado best," said Jeremy, "because it moves by bouncing, and laughs each time it lands. Bouncing is the only way a rubberado can get around."

"I feel sorry for the squonk," said Medora, "because it is always crying. If you catch a squonk and put it in a sack it will cry so hard that nothing is left but a puddle."

"Say, Pop," said Taylor, "did you know that kickle snifters live in old men's beards? They laugh all the time."

"Why do they laugh?" I asked.

"Because beards tickle," said Taylor.

"I like the wunk," said Joanna, "because when it gets scared it digs a hole, and jumps in, and pulls the hole in after it."

Alexander's choice was the goofus bird, which likes to see where it has been, so it flies backward. It also likes to sleep upside down. Elliott's favorite was the squidgicumsquee, which is as shy as the wunk. When something frightens it, it takes a deep breath and swallows itself.

Thank you, Mr. Schwartz.

14 November——————————————

Good Children and Bad

THE SNIFFLE

In spite of her sniffle
Isabel's chiffle.
Some girls with a sniffle
Would be weepy and tiffle;
They would look awful,
Like a rained-on waffle,
But Isabel's chiffle
In spite of her sniffle.
Her nose is more red
With a cold in her head,
But then, to be sure,
Her eyes are bluer.

Some girls with a snuffle,
Their tempers are uffle.
But when Isabel's snivelly
She's snivelly civilly,
And when she's snuffly
She's perfectly luffly.

—OGDEN NASH

15 November

BET YOU DIDN'T KNOW THAT!

In 1906, when people traveled by horse and buggy, the average speed of the traffic in midtown New York City was eleven and a half miles an hour. By 1972 the average speed of automobile traffic was down to eight miles an hour. It is probably less than that today.

Do you suppose traffic will stop altogether by the time you are grown?

16 November

TONGUE-TWISTER LIMERICKS

A canner exceedingly canny
One morning remarked to his granny
  "A canner can can
  Anything that he can,
But a canner can't can a can, can he?"

A tutor who tooted the flute
Tried to tutor two tooters to toot.
  Said the two to the tutor,
  "Is it harder to toot, or
To tutor two tooters to toot?"

—CAROLYN WELLS

17 November

PUNCTUATION PUZZLES

Everything in the sentence that follows is right except for the punctuation. Change the punctuation, without shifting a single word, so that the sentence will make sense. (See 23 October.)

When I was looking out the window, I saw a fire engine climbing a wall; I saw a swallow drinking soda; I saw a baby bigger than a house; I saw the sun as green as cheese; I saw the grass drinking beer; I saw two old men as drunk as I.

The meaning of the two sentences below changes with the punctuation:

A clever dog knows its master.
A clever dog knows it's master.

Do not break your bread, or roll in your soup.
Do not break your bread or roll in your soup.

18 November———————————

Thirty Purple Birds

Some New Yorkers used to say "erster" for "oyster" and "boid" for "bird."
This verse shows how they talked:*

> Coina Toid and Toity-toid
> Toity doity poiple boids
> Sittin' on the coib
> Eatin' woims
> And choipin' and boipin'.
>
> Along came Moitl
> And her goil friend Goitie.
> Boy, were they p'toibed.**

*W. M. Pinkerton heard his schoolmates recite this poem when he was a child. The first line, though, is his own creation.
** *P'toibed:* perturbed, upset.

19 November———————————

Googol

In the 1940s, an American mathematician named Edward Kasner asked his nine-year-old nephew, Milton Sirotta, to give a name to the number 1 followed by one hundred zeroes. "Googol," suggested Milton. That unimaginably huge number is now officially a *googol*. And the unimaginably large number of 10 raised to the power googol—which means 1 followed by ten zeros squared a hundred times—is a *googolplex*.

20 November—————————————————————

Vile Vodka

There was once an English racehorse whose name was spelled Potooooooooo.
It was pronounced *Pot-8-o's*—Potatoes. That is the way you should pronounce potooooooooo in the first line of this verse. But the oooooooooooo in
the third line is harder to solve; when you count the *o*'s, they come to eleven,
and eleven *o*'s do not make a sensible word. All right. Think again. There
were eight *o*'s run together in the first line, and eleven in the third. Eleven
o's are *more o*'s than eight *o*'s, aren't they? Now all you have to do is think of
a word that sounds like "more *o*'s." (The word means "gloomy, ill-hu-
mored.")

> Who of vodka distilled from potoooooooooo partakes
>   Should take warning:
> He'll be jolly at night, but oooooooooooo when he wakes
>   In the morning.
>   —W.R.E.

21 November—————————————————————

One day Little Audrey was standing on the corner just acrying and acrying,
when along came a cop who said, "Little Audrey, why are you crying?" And
Little Audrey said, "Oh, I've lost my papa!" The cop said, "Why, Little
Audrey, I wouldn't cry about that. There's your papa right across the street,
leaning against that bank building." Little Audrey was overjoyed; without
even looking at the traffic she started across the street. Along came a big
two-ton truck that ran over Little Audrey and killed her dead. The cop just
laughed and laughed. He knew all the time that that was not Little Audrey's
papa leaning against the bank building.

———•———

One day Little Audrey was playing with matches. Her mama said,
"Ummm, you better not do that." But Little Audrey was awfully hard-
headed; she kept right on playing with matches, and after a while she set the
house on fire, and it burned right down to the ground. Mama and Little
Audrey were looking at the ashes, and mama said, "Uh huh, I told you so!
Now, young lady, just wait until your papa comes home. You certainly will
catch it!" Little Audrey just laughed and laughed. She knew all the time that
papa had come home an hour early and had gone to bed to take a nap.

22 November————————————————————

A Tired Song of Tired Similes

When you say someone is "as ugly as sin," or runs "faster than the wind," or "sighs like a furnace," you are using a figure of speech called a simile, which compares something with something else by the use of the words *as, than,* or *like.* Here is a verse made up of similes:

As mute as a mackerel, darling, I am;
Yet fit as a fiddle, dear, gay as a lamb;
As clean as a whistle, as ugly as sin;
As fat as a hog, but as neat as a pin;
As brave as a lion, as deaf as an adder;
As brown as a berry, as mad as a hatter.

While you, my own darling, the love of my life,
Are free as the wind, and as sharp as a knife;
As blind as a bat and as sly as a fox,
As pert as a sparrow, as dumb as an ox;
As plump as a partridge, as red as a rose,
As flat as a flounder, as plain as my nose.

So come, let us marry!—We two shall be twain,
As merry as crickets, and righter than rain!
Our days will be brighter than rainbows are bright;
Our hearts will be lighter than feathers are light.
Our love will be surer than shooting is sure,
And we shall be poorer than churchmice are poor.

—W.R.E.

23 November————————————————————

Wow, Hannah!

I've talked about sentences that read the same forward or backward—"Rise to vote, sir," for instance. There are also hundreds of *words* that read the same either way. How many can you find in the story below?

"Wow!" said Hannah, "look at the sun, over there behind that radar tower. It looks redder than it did at noon."

"It sure does, ma'am," exclaimed Otto, bending over to pat the head of a small brown pup with black markings over one eye.

HAVE ANGLEWORMS ATTRACTIVE HOMES?

Have Angleworms attractive homes?
> Do Bumble-bees have brains?
Do Caterpillars carry combs?
> Do Dodos dote on drains?
Can Eels elude elastic earls?
> Do Flatfish fish for flats?
Are Grigs agreeable to girls?
> Do Hares have hunting-hats?
Do ices make an Ibex ill?
> Do Jackdaws jug their jam?
Do Kites kiss all the kids they kill?
> Do Llamas live on lamb?
Will Moles molest a mounted mink?
> Do Newts deny the news?
Are Oysters boisterous when they drink?
> Do Parrots prowl in pews?
Do Quakers get their quills from Quails?
> Do Rabbits rob on roads?
Are Snakes supposed to sneer at Snails?
> Do Tortoises tease Toads?
Can Unicorns perform on horns?
> Do Vipers value veal?
Do Weasels weep when fast asleep?
> Can Xylophagans squeal?
Do Yaks in packs invite attacks?
> Are Zebras full of zeal?
> > —CHARLES E. CARRYL

Nicknames Unnicked

Many common words come from nicknames. What would the words look like if the real name was used instead?

Well, instead of tomboy, tomcat, tommyrot, you would have Thomasboy, Thomascat, Thomasrot.

Instead of magpie you would have Margaretpie; instead of nanny goat, Ann goat; instead of paddy wagon, Patrick wagon; instead of chuck wagon, Charles wagon.

Jack would be John. You would have bootjohn, Johnknife, John-in-the-pulpit, John-of-all-trades, hijohn, and skyjohn.

A brown betty would be a brown Elizabeth. A good-time charley would be a good-time Charles. A teddy bear would be a Theodore bear.

(The "chuck" in chuck wagon is really from "chock;" it means a cut of beef. Other words that *sound* as if they came from nicknames, but don't, are penny ante and Dutch bob. What if you called them Penelope ante and Dutch Robert?)

26 November

Bactrian Camels Have Two Humps

As you read this verse, keep in mind that Siam is the former name of Thailand; that Campbellites are members of a religious sect; that a Bactrian camel has two humps; and that uberous means "supplying milk in abundance."

> I met on a tram in exotic Siam
>> (Known as *tramela* out in Siamela)
> Three Campbellite camels—a sire, dam,
>>> and lamb
>> (In Siamese, *Camela famila*).
>
> The sire was Ben-Amelek Ben-Abraham,
> A curious name for a Bactrian cam,
>> (Which is Siamese shorthand for *camela*).
> Ma'am Ben-Abraham was a well-trodden dam
> (Whom tram-trippers taunted as Bactrius mam
>> On account of her uberous *mammilla*)
> Who suckled a Campbellite camel named Pam
>> (Though sometimes she answered to Pamela).
>
> And what has becam of that *Camela* fam
> Since they traveled away on their Siamese tram,
> I've never been told, and I don't give a damn,
>> Or even a Siamese *dammela*.
>>> —W.R.E.

206

27 November —————————————————

Can you figure out these rebuses?

1. | Stand | take | 2 | takings |
   |-------|------|-----|---------|
   | I | you | throw | my |

2. | | | B | | |
   |--------|-----|----------|------|--------|
   | Faults | man | quarrels | wife | faults |

3. | Father |
   |--------|
   | I am |

28 November —————————————————

THE PYGMY RACE WERE LITTLE MANS*

The Pygmy race were little mans,
Never taller than three spans.
*(Also they had pygmy brains
Not to know those giant Cranes
Could whip them standing on one leg,
And still take time to lay an egg.)*
— W.R.E.

*Mythology says the Pygmies were but three spans tall. Three spans is twenty-seven inches. They fought a bitter war with the Cranes, and were finally destroyed.

29 November

JEREMY: Did your watch stop when it hit the floor?
ALEXANDER: Naturally. You didn't think it would go through, did you?

ELLIOTT: I forgot my gloves.
MEDORA: Why didn't you tie a string around your finger?
ELLIOTT: A string wouldn't keep my hands warm.

ALEXANDER: If I cut a steak into four parts, what do I have?
ELLIOTT, JEREMY, and MEDORA: Quarters.
ALEXANDER: And if I cut those pieces in half again?
ELLIOTT, JEREMY, and MEDORA: Eighths.
ALEXANDER: And again?
ELLIOTT, JEREMY, and MEDORA: Sixteenths.
ALEXANDER: And what will I get if I do it once more?
ELLIOTT, JEREMY, and MEDORA: Hash!

30 November

*No, It Doesn't**

When Elliott was a kindergarten student, he went to and from school in a bus that had overhead bars for the older children to hold onto. Elliott used these as monkey bars, hanging from them upside down. Now that he is a big fellow of ten, he no longer travels upside down, but sometimes he still has an upside-down way of thinking. In fact he tried to convince Medora today that up and down mean the same thing.

"No, they don't," said Medora.

"Yes, they do. 'Burn it up' means the same as 'burn it down,'" said Elliott.

"And 'tie him up' means the same as 'tie him down,'" added Jeremy, who likes to agree with Elliott.

"'On' means the same as 'off,'" said Elliott.

"No, it doesn't," said Alexander.

"Yes, it does. 'What's going on?' means the same as 'What's coming off?'" said Elliott.

And he was right, too.

*Thanks to Cecil K. Stedman

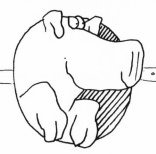

December

1 December

DECEMBER

Whether DECEMBER is better or worse,
It's the last month I need to put into a verse.

—W.R.E.

IN THE LAND OF SILLY

Come let us walk
    In the land of Silly,
Where we can talk
    In Piccalilli:
Molly-coddle, spick-and-span,

Helter-skelter, catamaran,
    Willy-nilly,
    Daffy-dilly,
That's how we'll talk
    In the land of Silly.

—W.R.E.

2 December

The First Christmas Tree

The fourth Sunday before Christmas is the beginning of Advent for Christians. Many fast and pray during these four weeks. Mala Powers tells a story like the following one for each day of Advent.

On a dark and wintry night, nearly 1,200 years ago, Winfred, the Englishman, strode into a large clearing, deep in a forest in northern Germany. Gathered in the clearing were tribesmen who worshiped nature and made human sacrifices at the foot of a giant oak called the Blood Oak. Their high priest was holding a young boy whom he was about to sacrifice to the Norse god Thor.

As the high priest raised his stone hammer to strike, Winfred rushed across the clearing and intercepted the blow with his staff. Then, before the astonished eyes of the tribesmen, he drew forth a wooden cross and touched the giant tree. Instantly the Blood Oak split in two and crashed to the ground.

Just behind the fallen oak stood a young fir tree, pointing toward the heavens. "This little evergreen shall be your holy tree tonight," Winfred told them. "It is a sign of endless life, for its leaves are always green."

Then he told them of the birth of the Baby Jesus in Bethlehem and of the gift of love and mercy which Christ brought to all mankind.

And all who listened were filled with awe and wonder. They called the evergreen "the tree of the Christ Child" and hung gifts upon its branches. And the light of the moon made the tree sparkle until it seemed to be tangled full of stars. And hymns of thanks were sung for the Babe of Bethlehem.

KNOCK KNOCKS

3 December

JEREMY: Knock knock.
JOANNA: Who's there?
JEREMY: Gorilla.
JOANNA: Gorilla who?
JEREMY: Gorilla my dreams, I love you.

JOANNA: Knock knock.
JEREMY: Who's there?
JOANNA: Sharon.
JEREMY: Sharon who?
JOANNA: Sharon share alike.

MEDORA: Knock knock.
TAYLOR: Who's there?
MEDORA: Carmen.
TAYLOR: Carmen who?
MEDORA: Carmen get it!

MEDORA: Knock knock.
TAYLOR: Who's there?
MEDORA: Celia.
TAYLOR: Celia who?
MEDORA: Celia later.

COUNTING RHYMES

4 December

Jeremy's Counting-out Rhymes

Hickety pickety i sillickety
Pomalorum jig,
Every man who has no hair
Generally wears a wig.
One, two, three,
Out goes he.

Oh, deary me,
Mother caught a flea,
Put it in the kettle
To make a cup of tea.
The flea jumped out,
And bit mother's snout,
In came daddy
With his shirt hanging out.
O-U-T spells out.

SKIP ROPE RHYME

Have a cigarette, sir?
No, sir.
Why, sir?
Because I've got a cold, sir.
Where did you catch the cold, sir?
Up at the North Pole, sir.
What were you doing there, sir?
Shooting polar bears, sir.
How many did you shoot, sir?
One, two, three, four, five . . .

5 December———————————————— JUMBLED GEOG- RAPHY

CHAIN STATES

Wyoming is in Kent County, Delaware;
Delaware is in Southampton County, Virginia;
Virginia is in Kitsap County, Washington;
Washington is in Knox County, Maine;
Maine is in Coconino County, Arizona;
Arizona is in Burt County, Nebraska;
Nebraska is in Jennings County, Indiana;
Indiana is in Indiana County, Pennsylvania;
Pennsylvania is in Mobile County, Alabama;
Alabama is in Genesee County, New York;
New York is in Santa Rosa County, Florida;
Florida is in Houghton County, Michigan;
Michigan is in Osage County, Kansas;
Kansas is in Seneca County, Ohio;
Ohio is in Gunnison County, Colorado;

Colorado is in South Central District, Alaska;
Alaska is in Mineral County, West Virginia;
West Virginia is in St. Louis County, Minnesota;
Minnesota is in Colquitt County, Georgia;
Georgia is in Lamar County, Texas;
Texas is in Baltimore County, Maryland;
Maryland is in East Baton Rouge County, Louisiana;
Louisiana is in Pike County, Missouri;
Missouri is in Brown County, Illinois;
Illinois is in Sequoyah County, Oklahoma;
Oklahoma is in Daviess County, Kentucky.

—DARRYL FRANCIS

LIMERICKS **6 December**————————————————

The nose of Tante Rose is supreme—
Her sneezes start earthquakes in Nîmes.
     Her friends and her foes
     Rent the bridge of her nose
When they need to cross over a stream.

—W.R.E.

Douglas MacPherson MacPhee
Is an elegant sight on TV.
     Once I happened to meet
     Him crossing the street—
He looked just as common as me.

—W.R.E.

ANIMALS **7 December**————————————————

Oh, Mongoose!

A man wrote a letter asking a pet store for two mongooses. But the word did not look right, so he changed it to two mongeese. That did not look right either, so he wrote, "Please send me one mongoose. And while you are at it, send me another one."

   If the plural of mongoose is hard to remember, the names that distinguish the young of one kind of animal from the young of another kind are even harder:

ANIMAL OFFSPRING

A cow has a calf, but the calf of a mare
Is a colt, and a cub is the colt of a bear;
A fawn is the cub of a deer, while the fawn
Of a beaver's a kitten, and, carrying on,
The kit of a sheep is a lamb, and the lamb
Of a wolf is a whelp, while the whelp of madame
Is a babe, and the babe of a dog is a pup,
And I thought for awhile this would wind the thing up,
But the pup of a goat is a kid, and, *Mon Dieu!*
A joey's the kid of a kangkangaroo.

—W.R.E.

8 December

Sugar, Yes . . . but Spice?

Sugar and spice and everything nice—that's what little girls are made of.

Well, says John Schell in *Reader's Digest*, sugar anyhow. A girl is also made of enough chlorine to disinfect five swimming pools; eighty-five pounds of oxygen; two ounces of salt; fifty quarts of water; three pounds of calcium; twenty-four pounds of carbon; enough phosphorus for ten bars of soap; enough iron to make a sixpenny nail; enough sulfur to rid a dog of fleas; and enough glycerine to explode an artillery shell.

But Mr. Schell found no spice at all.

(How much did that little girl weigh, do you suppose?)

AUTOBIOGRAPHY

Sometimes I'm nasty, mean and cross,
And bother my brother, and act as boss,
And gen'rally behave like a nasty brat;
—And sometimes I'm not as nice as that!

—PAUL E. MANHEIM

9 December————————————————

A THOUGHT*

It is very nice to know
    That I am made so neatly,
And that my little skin and bones
    Cover me completely.
For I should blush for very shame
    If when I was a-thinking
My skin and bones should come undone
    And leave my mind a-blinking,
And all my wicked thoughts and feelings
    Naked in the light.
Oh, I'm extremely glad to feel
    My fastenings are tight.
        —DOROTHY ALDIS

*Dotty Hillman sent this.

10 December————————————————

Dooley's Hats

This morning a Christmas card came in the mail from Will Shortz, the only man alive with a college degree in word puzzles. The card was a puzzle in which Will and nine friends stand in a circle, facing inward. Each wears a hat with a word on it, so that everybody can see all the words except his own. Each person is supposed to figure out the word on his own hat by pairing the words on the other hats and seeing what's left. The words that Will sees are *tennis, paint, white, grease, off, elbow, brush, table,* and *card.*

What is the word on Will's hat?

To find out, he looks for a relationship among the words. He notices that *tennis* and *elbow* go together—tennis elbow. And *elbow* goes with *grease*—elbow grease. And *paint* goes with *brush*—paint brush. He quickly fits the other words into natural pairs, until there is only one word left. That has to be the companion word to the one on his hat. And because the game was announced as a holiday puzzle, he knows his word has to be—what?

It took Alexander two minutes to figure out the answer. See how long it takes you.

11 December———————————— NONSENSE

KINDNESS TO ANIMALS

Speak gently to the herring and kindly to the calf,
Be blithesome with the bunny, at barnacles don't laugh!
Give nuts unto the monkey, and buns unto the bear,
Ne'er hint at currant jelly if you chance to see a hare!
Oh, little girls, pray hide your combs when tortoises
    draw nigh,
And never in the hearing of a pigeon whisper pie!
But give the stranded jellyfish a shove into the sea—
Be always kind to animals wherever you may be!

Be lenient with lobsters, and ever kind to crabs,
And be not disrespectful to cuttlefish or dabs;
Chase not the Cochin China, chaff not the ox obese,
And babble not of feather beds in company with geese.
Be tender with the tadpole, and let the limpet thrive,
Be merciful to mussels, don't skin your eels alive;
When talking to a turtle don't mention calipee—
Be always kind to animals wherever you may be.
                —J. ASHBY-STERRY

12 December———————————— IN THE FOREIGN FASHION

K and O (with a Little N Thrown In)

It is too bad that the letter *n* slipped once into this Finnish conversation; otherwise it would use only the letters *k* and *o*.*

    Kokoo kokoon koko kokko . . .
    Koko kokkoko?
    Koko kokko.
It means:
    Gather together the wherewithal for a bonfire.
    A whole wherewithal?
    A whole wherewithal.

By the way, the Finnish word for "soap salesman" is a palindrome, reading the same both ways: *saippuakauppias.*

*Trudy Wolcott sent me this wordplay.

13 December————————————————

L
O
L
L
Y
P
O
P

—RICHARD KOSTELANETZ

14 December————————————————

"*Podium* is simply a form of *pew*" —TV quiz.

IN LODIUM

They said it was a podium,
      A podium or pew;
A thing I never knodium,
      I never, never knew.
Which controversial vodium,
      Or questionable view,
Intelligence must rodium,
      Must rodium or rue;
And treat with scornful odium,
Or take with grain of sodium,
With grains of chloride sodium,
And not of these a fodium,
      A fodium or few.

Whoever wrote the poem knew that a podium is *not* simply a form of pew. A pew is a bench for the congregation in a church. A podium is an elevated platform for a speaker or orchestra conductor.

15 December————————————— PUNS

Medora and Jeremy sometimes recite this verse, maybe because they are taking piano lessons:

MEDORA: Why piccolo profession
           Like music
           That's full of viol practices
           Confirmed lyres
           Old fiddles
           And bass desires?
JEREMY: For the lute, of course.

—ALAN F. G. LEWIS

16 December————————————— ANGUISH LANGUISH

Ant Song

The story on 3 July is told in combinations of letters that when read out loud sound *almost* like real words. In the verse that follows, the words are all wrong, but they sound *exactly* like the right ones.

Necks tweak coffer mere Rome ants
Holed mead ants and ants and ants
Ants sir ants sir ants Urdu
Lettuce turnip pay sore too.

—W.R.E.

17 December————————————— CRAZY LOGIC

Paradoxes

A paradox is a statement that seems contradictory, but may be true. These are paradoxes:

- To walk down the street is to walk up the street.
- Since the hour hand is the first hand on a clock, and the minute hand is the second hand, the second hand is the third hand.
- To fill out a form is to fill it in.
- A near miss is a near hit.
- A boxing ring is square.
- A slim chance is the same as a fat chance.
- When the bases are loaded, a walk is a run.

18 December————————————

The Shortest Verse

Of short-short verses, the most famous is:

> Adam
> Had 'em.

This is supposed to mean that Adam had fleas, or perhaps bedbugs—though it may refer to his sons Cain and Abel.

The verse that follows is, I think, as short as a verse can get. To understand it, though, you have to know that T in ABC language stands for tea, and that C in Spanish ABC language (if the Spanish play with ABC language) stands for *si*, which is Spanish for yes. And you have to read a very, very long title.

A Genteel Exchange Between the British Ambassador's Wife, Who Speaks No Spanish, and the Spanish Ambassador's Wife, Who Speaks No English, During an Afternoon Call on the Former by the Latter; Written for Those with Some Knowledge of English, Spanish, and the Language of ABC:

> "T?"
> "C."

—W.R.E.

19 December————————————

DID YOU EVER, EVER, EVER

Did you ever, ever, ever,
   In your leaf, life, loaf,
See the deevel, divil, dovol,
   Kiss his weef, wife, woaf?

No, I never, never, never,
   In my leaf, life, loaf,
Saw the deevel, divil, dovol,
   Kiss his weef, wife, woaf.

Hang your serious songs, said Sipsop and he sang as follows:

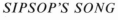

SIPSOP'S SONG

Fa ra so bo ro
   Fa ra bo ra
Sa ba ra ra rare roro
Sa ra ra ra bo ro ro ro
Radara
Sarpodo no flo ro
—WILLIAM BLAKE

20 December————————————————

- Be it ever so hovel, there's no place like home.
- I got up at the crank of dawn.
- We are all cremated equal.
- I refused to tell him who I was—I used a facetious name.
- The food in that restaurant is abdominal.
- Explain it to me in words of one cylinder.
- Congress is still in season.
- All of Abe Lincoln's pictures make him look so thin and emancipated.

—GOODMAN ACE

21 December————————————————

I WOT WHAT NOT

Of all the dates I wis one wert
   of all dates most unkind
Which wert the date comes up the street
   with the date you leave behind

Of all the dukes to shake I wis
   one wert no shakes to meet
Which wert I wot now how he stands
   and wis not where his feet.

—EWART MILNE

22 December————————————————

At Christmas, What Happens to Friday?

Christmas is recognized even by people who are not Christians. The Communists who run Czechoslovakia, for instance, despise all religions; but Christmas is still a legal holiday there. Sometimes the Communist officials in Czechoslovakia appear to be confused about how Christmas fits into the days of the week. One year they released these holiday instructions to the workers:

> Because Christmas Eve will fall on a Thursday, that day will be considered a Saturday for work purposes. Factories will be closed all day, although stores will remain closed a half day only. Friday, December 25, will be considered a Sunday, with both factories and stores open all day. Monday, December 28, will be a Wednesday for work purposes. Wednesday will be a business Friday. Saturday will be a Sunday, and Sunday will be a Monday.

23 December————————————————

Decorating the Tree

The children were helping me decorate the Christmas tree. The way they helped was to hang the bells and globes and angels and icicles, and to arrange the lights and garlands. My job was to sit in my easy chair and find fault.

"Jeremy," I said, "move that angel closer to the green bulb. . . . Medora, don't you think there should be more lights next to the trunk?"

"Pop," said Elliott, "Taylor saw a crèche in a department store yesterday, and do you know what he said? He said, 'Oh, look at the infant Jesus and the Three Wise Guys!' "

"Did not," said Taylor.

"Do you remember Clement Moore's poem about the night before Christmas?" I asked. "How many times do you think Santa Claus is mentioned?"

Alexander said five, and Medora said eight.

"Santa Claus is not mentioned even once," I said triumphantly. "The title of the poem is *A Visit from Saint Nicholas,* and Santa is never referred to at all—Saint Nick is. All right—now I'll ask you something else. Have you ever heard that it is wrong and disrespectful to spell Christmas *Xmas?*"

"I read that someplace," said Alexander.

"Well, it's *not* wrong. The Greek word for Christ begins with the letter *chi,* which we call X. And X stands for the cross, too."

"Gee, Pop, how do you know so much?" asked Elliott.

I hesitated only a moment before admitting that I had just been reading about Christmas in Norman Hickman's *The Quintessential Quiz Book.*

The least I can do is be honest with my grandchildren.

24 December————————————————

Mistletoe

Kissing under the mistletoe is an old Christmas custom. But oh, dear—the word *mistletoe* combines two words meaning "dung" and "twig," and the mistletoe was first believed to spring from the droppings of birds. It is something to bear in mind the next time you see somebody waiting, with puckered lips, to be kissed beneath the mistletoe.

25 December

The Birth of Christ

And so it was, that, while they were there, the days were accomplished that she should be delivered.

And she brought forth her firstborn son, and wrapped him in swaddling clothes, and laid him in a manger; because there was no room for them in the inn.

And there were in the same country shepherds abiding in the field, keeping watch over their flock by night.

And, lo, the angel of the Lord came upon them, and the glory of the Lord shone round about them; and they were sore afraid.

And the angel said unto them, Fear not: for, behold, I bring you good tidings of great joy, which shall be to all people.

For unto you is born this day in the city of David a Saviour, which is Christ the Lord.

And this *shall be* a sign unto you; Ye shall find the babe wrapped in swaddling clothes, lying in a manger.

And suddenly there was with the angel a multitude of the heavenly host praising God, and saying,

Glory to God in the highest, and on earth peace, good will toward men.

And it came to pass, as the angels were gone away from them into heaven, the shepherds said one to another. Let us now go even unto Bethlehem, and see this thing which is come to pass, which the Lord hath made known unto us.

And they came with haste, and found Mary, and Joseph, and the babe lying in a manger.

—LUKE 2:6–16

26 December

NONSENSE

Rub-a-dub-dub, dear,
  My heart goes, all agog
That you are drawing near—
  Hot diggety-dog!

When you are passing by,
  I hippety-hippety-hop;
And if I catch your eye,
  I snap, crackle, pop.

—W.R.E.

A doctor fell in a deep well
And broke his collarbone.
The moral: Doctor, mind the sick
And let the well alone.

27 December ————————————————————————

Who Is Who?

I said, "How smart are you, Elliott?"

"Very smart," said Elliott.

"But not as smart as me," said Alexander.

"Or me," said Jeremy.

"Very well," I said. "Here is a puzzle. Three men work in a store. Their names are the same as yours—Alexander, Elliott, and Jeremy. One is the manager. One is the salesclerk. One is the deliveryman. You have to decide which is which. The deliveryman, who is an only child, earns the least. Elliott, who married Jeremy's sister, earns more than the salesclerk. Which man has which job?"

Alexander rubbed his chin. He said, "Jeremy has a sister, but the deliveryman is an only child. So the deliveryman is not Jeremy. He is either Alexander or Elliott."

Jeremy said, "But Elliott earns most, and the deliveryman earns least, so the deliveryman is not Elliott. He is Alexander."

"But which one is the salesclerk, and which one the manager?"

"Elliott earns more than the salesclerk," said Jeremy, "so he is not the salesclerk and since he is not the deliveryman, he must be the manager."

"And the salesclerk," cried all three together, "is Jeremy!"

28 December ————————————————————————

SCIENCE FOR THE YOUNG

Arthur with a lighted taper
Touched the fire to grandpa's paper.
Grandpa leaped a foot or higher,
Dropped the sheet and shouted, "Fire!"
Arthur, wrapped in contemplation,
Viewed the scene of conflagration.
"This," he said, "confirms my notion—
Heat creates both light and motion."

Wee, experimental Nina
Dropped her mother's Dresden china
From a seventh-story casement,
Smashing, crashing to the basement.
Nina, somewhat apprehensive,
Said, "This china is expensive,
Yet it proves by demonstration
Newton's law of gravitation."
—WALLACE IRWIN

29 December —————————————————— COUNTRY MUSIC

If You Want to Keep the Beer Real Cold

Alexander has not yet begun to show an interest in girls, but it won't be long now. Already he is singing a country song that contains the line "If you want to keep the beer real cold, put it next to my ex-wife's heart." Here are lines adapted from other country songs, with apologies and thanks to the original lyricists:*

Forever wasn't quite as long as I had counted on;
I've been a long time leaving, but I'll be a long
time gone.

She's just a name dropper, and she's dropping mine;
If I was a fish, I would cut off the line.

We swore, "For better or for worse," and we were
not far wrong;
We swore for better or for worse, but not for very long.

You left your footprints on my stomach when you walked
out of my heart.

You're the hangnail in my life, and I can't bite you off.

*The first three selections were collected by Doug Todd, and were called to my attention by Dr. Leslie L. Nunn. James H. Rhodes sent the last two.

30 December

I HAD A LITTLE BROTHER

I had a little brother, his name was Tiny Tim,
I put him in the bathtub to teach him how to swim.
He drank up all the water; he ate up all the soap;
He tried to eat the bathtub, but it wouldn't go down his throat.
My mother called the doctor;
The doctor called his nurse;
The nurse called the lady with the alligator purse.
"Mumps," said the doctor,
"Mumps," said the nurse.
"Mumps," said the lady with the alligator purse.
Out went the doctor, *out* went the nurse,
Out went the lady with the baby in her purse.

IF YOU EVER

If you ever ever ever ever ever
    If you ever ever ever meet a whale
You must never never never never never
    You must never never never touch its tail:
For if you ever ever ever ever ever,
    If you ever ever ever touch its tail,
You will never never never never never
    You will never never meet another whale.

31 December

Ode to an Elevator

Alexander and Elliott and Medora and Jeremy and Joanna and Taylor came calling today to wish me Happy New Year. Afterward they went to a New Year's Eve party, and I saw them off at the elevator. We waited and we w-a-i-t-e-d and we w–a–i–t–e–d for the elevator to arrive. Then I went back to my desk to write this verse.

Capricious, upsy-downsy sweet,
    My patience with thy presence crown!
Pray, when thy rising I entreat,
No more, dear love, rush past my feet
    Down!

Behold thy button burning bright,
    A signal thou wilt be here soon—
If not today, if not tonight,
Some other day, when clappers smite
    Noon.

I hear thee coming! Praise to thee,
    And praise to God, and praise to luck!—
(Though well I know that presently,
'Twixt Six and Seven, I shall be
    Stuck.)

Thy door slides open. Slightly squiffed,
    I sense too late the empty draft.
A lesser lover would be miffed
To find no lift,* but only lift
    Shaft.

I pray thee no salt tears to shed;
    I pray thee, drink no hemlock cup.**
But I adjure thee, since I'm dead,
When next I press thy button, head
    Up.

                              —W.R.E.

HAPPY NEW YEAR—and I hope you never have to wait that long for an elevator!

*The English call elevators lifts.
**Hemlock is the deadly poison that Socrates drank when he was sentenced to death by the Athenians.

Answers and Solutions

7 January

1. None. The tree grows plums.
2. Volume nine
3. They will never be under water. As the tide rises, so will the ship and the ladder.
4. The two very thin women cross in the boat. One comes back and the very fat woman takes the boat across. Then the second very thin woman comes back in the boat and picks up the first very thin woman.
5. About 200

17 January

3. Dusk, tusk, Turk, lurk, lark, dark, darn, dawn
4. East, last, lest, west
5. Hate, have, lave, love
6. Heat, head, herd, here, hire, fire
7. Lead, load, goad, gold
8. Lion, loon, boon, boor, boar, bear

(Can you do these in fewer words?)

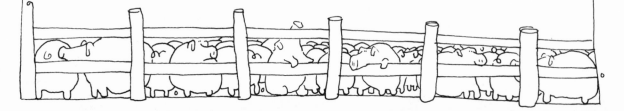

19 January

1. *Only* I hit him in the eye yesterday. That is, I was the only one who hit him.
2. I *only* hit him in the eye yesterday. That is, the only thing I did was hit him in the eye.
3. I hit *only* him in the eye yesterday. That is, I hit no one else.
4. I hit him *only* in the eye yesterday. That is, I hit him nowhere else.
5. I hit him in the *only* eye yesterday. That is, he had but one eye.
6. I hit him in the eye *only* yesterday. That is, I hit him in the eye as recently as yesterday.
7. I hit him in the eye yesterday *only*. That is, yesterday was the only day I hit him in the eye.

28 January

1. Much ado about nothing.   2. World without end, amen.
3. Frameup.   4. All in one.   5. Square meal.

29 January

Oh, I see you are empty!

6 February

Diamrab is barmaid spelled backward. *Tseug* is guest spelled backward. *Nerdlihc* is children spelled backward. *Tse* is est spelled backward. So the verse reads:

> A *backward barmaid* fell in love
> And wed her *backward guest.*
> Of all earth's *backward children*
> Theirs were the *backwardest.*

8 February

(1) Wash. (2) Ark. (3) Pa. (4) Me. (5) O. (6) Md. (7) Miss. (8) Mass. (9) Tenn. (10) Ala. (11) Penn. (12) Del.

16 February

(1) Burma (2) Ceylon (3) Taiwan (4) China (5) Tibet (6) Athens (7) Iceland (8) Iran (9) South Korea (10) Japan

21 February

1. Revolution. A *revolution* is a momentous change; a *resolution* is a decision to do something.
2. Feather
3. Tycoon. A *tycoon* is a wealthy and powerful man; a *typhoon* is a severe tropical hurricane in the western Pacific.
4. Busybody
5. Under, of course
6. Mascara
7. Elevator
8. Forceps. *Forceps* is an instrument resembling a pair of tongs. *Biceps* is the large muscle at the front of your upper arm.

2 March

1. Loving shepherd
2. "Conquering Kings Their Titles Take"
3. Half-formed wish

5 March

There are several ways of punctuating the "said" puzzle, depending on where you wish to use the name of the city, which I capitalize here for quick identification:

Said I, "I said you said I said 'said'." Said he, "Who said I said you said 'said'? I said SAID is said SAID. SAID is not said 'said'."

9 March

"Abey, have you any eggs?
"Yes we have eggs."
"Have you any ham?"
"Yes we have ham."
"OK, I'll have ham and eggs."

10 March

There are ten *der*'s in the first line, ten *der*'s in the second line, and ten *der*'s in the fourth line. So the verse reads:

> So tender's the night,
> So tender's the voice of the dove,
> That a fellow's quite right
> If he tenders his lady his love.

16 March

(1) Ostrich (2) Bear (3) Beaver (4) Horse (5) Eel (6) Worm (7) Lion (8) Dog

4 April

1. He fell between two stools.   2. I ate that apple.

9 April

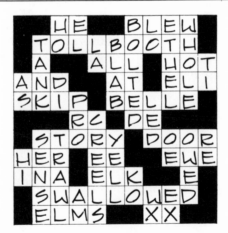

14 April

1. He got tired of the "hole" business.
2. In the dictionary
3. When they make 88
4. Alphabet
5. A quartet
6. The word *wrong*
7. On his head
8. None. A hole is empty.

18 April

Turn 710 upside down and you will see that the answer is OIL.

$$710 \quad OIL$$

20 April

(1) Number (2) Pounds (3) Space (in proofreading) (4) Sharp (in music) (5) Tic-tac-toe (6) Octothorp (7) Non-add (i.e. do not add the following number) (8) Fracture (of a bone) (9) Delimiter. (Mark Burstein, Warden of the West Coast Chapter of the Lewis Carroll Society of North America, informs me that in certain computer languages a delimiter is used to signify the logical end of a line of code, much as a period signifies the end of a sentence. Or it may hold the place for data yet to be filled in: ##/##/## in computer code might appear in the decoded report as, say, 08/06/41. I *think* I understand this, and I am sure *you* will.)

(Octothorp is the # on a push-button telephone. Rumor at the telephone company is that a man named Charles B. Octothorp, wanting to make his name famous, would approach anyone with a Touch-Tone 'phone, stop, and say admiringly, "That's a mighty handsome octothorp you have there." Whether or not that story is true, the telephone company now prefers that you call a # a "number sign." Lots of people still say "octothorp," though.)

29 April

The bat flies in, the bat flies out;
He *lifts* his wings, and *flits* about.

"*Snip!*" go the scissors;
"*Spin!*" goes the top.
Jane *pins* her skirt on;
The dog *nips* the cop.

30 April

A whip   A book

14 May

Deer, dear; hare, hair; hart, heart; barely, bear, bear
Plain, plane; pair, pears; rake, rake; tear, tares
Beer, bier; coughing, coffin; ale, ail
Quails, quail; bough, bow; rein, rain, reigns

21 May

1. Old Mother Hubbard went to the cupboard to get her poor dog a bone.
2. Diddle diddle dumpling my son John.
3. There was a little man and he had a little gun.
4. Wee Willy Winkie runs through the town.
5. Simple Simon met a pieman going to the fair.

29 May

1. "Is the dean busy?"
2. "I have never before addressed so many sons of toil."
3. . . . he congratulated him on his "cozy little nook."
4. He hailed the "cheerful tidings" of the gospels, and asked the congregation to sing with him from "Greenland's Icy Mountains."

From H. Allen Smith:

1. "I'm getting my shoes half-soled after I have a cup of coffee."
2. "The plot thickens."
3. "The Indian died and went to the happy hunting ground."
4. "Give me a jar of underarm deodorant."

3 June

Somersault (summer, salt); sacred, scared; s(t)urgeon; the letter *r*.

14 June

TO EMILY

O, Emily, what ecstasy
I emanate* when you I see!
I used to rave of Ellen's eyes,
For Elsie I gave countless sighs;
For Katie, and for Eleanor
I was a keen competitor;
But each now's a nonentity,
For you excel them all you see.

Emanate means "send forth."

17 June

> Every lady in the land
>> Has twenty nails: on each hand,
> Five; and twenty on hands and feet.
>> This is true, without deceit.

That that is, is not that that is not; that that is not, is not that that is. Is that not it? It is.

21 June

The five airy creatures are five vowels: A, E, I, O, U. Why are they "airy"? Because they are made of air—the air that comes out of your throat.

2 July

(1) Keeps me awake (2) Battle-scarred veterans (3) Black Joe (4) Geese to fly

3 July

Our Father which art in heaven,
Hallowed be thy name.
Thy kingdom come, Thy will be done
In earth as it is in heaven.
Give us this day our daily bread,
And forgive us our debts,

As we forgive our debtors.
Lead us not into temptation,
But deliver us from evil,
For Thine is the kingdom,
The power, and the glory
Forever. Amen.

9 July

1. Stubborn as a mule.
2. A penny saved is a penny earned.
3. A man's best friend is his dog.
4. A bird in the hand is worth two in the bush.

15 July

Though my *tenant's* a lass who's a loner,
So many *contenders* are milling
About with *pretensions* to own her,
They'd be dear at *ten ha'pence* the shilling.

CHORUS: They'd be dear at, etc.

The *tendrils* that frame her sweet forehead
Would merit *Tenniel's* attention;
But her *tenement's* mine—and *I'm* horrid;
I jeer at romantic *intentions.*

CHORUS: I jeer at, etc.

If she *tenders* her payments I care not
How *tender's* this lass when unbent.
Treat *tenants* as human? I swear not:
Their *tendency's* not to pay rent.

CHORUS: Their *tendency's,* etc.

16 July

Sleeplessness

20 July

The Mrs. kissed her Mr.
Then how her Mr. kissed her!
He kissed her kissed her kissed her
Until he raised a blister.
The blister killed his Mrs.
Then how he missed her kisses!

He missed her missed her missed her
Until he kissed her sister.
He covered her with kisses
Till she became his Mrs.
The Mrs. kissed her Mr.
(and so on and on and on)

21 July

1. A stitch in time saves nine.
2. A bird in the hand is worth two in the bush.
3. Go further and do worse.
4. Early to bed and early to rise makes a man healthy, wealthy, and wise.
5. Better late than never.
6. All's well that ends well.

4 August

Maine, main, mane; Holy, holey, wholly; New, gnu, knew

6 August

8 August

The upper crust I call myself,
    A chap with cash to crow about;
I clip poor clucks of hard-earned pelf;
    I'm clever; I'm a cat with clout.

Though cranks may chide me, what care I?
    I live in clover; creed I've none.
I charm, I cheat, I also lie.
    A crook I may be—but I'm fun.

As I climb closer to my crest,
    Admit that I have class, old chap.
Don't cluck at me—I do my best;
    I'm close to perfect. Why not clap?

13 August

TO A SICK FRIEND

I'm in a tender mood today,
    And feel poetic, too;
For fun I'll just dash off a line
    And send it off to you.

I'm sorry you've been sick so long;
    Don't be disconsolate;
But bear your ills with fortitude,
    And they won't seem so great.

3 September

1. Facetiously   2. Abstemiously   3. Arseniously

4 September

1. A cup of coffee
2. An order of Jell-O
3. French fried potatoes added
4. Corned beef and cabbage
5. Salt and pepper
6. Doughnut and coffee
7. A glass of buttermilk
8. Hash with catsup
9. A glass of water
10. A hot dog
11. An Italian hero sandwich
12. Bacon, lettuce, and tomato sandwich without mayonnaise
13. Beans with two frankfurters
14. Beef stew
15. Scrambled eggs with whole wheat toast
16. Vanilla ice cream in a chocolate soda or milkshake (sometimes also coffee with cream)
17. A glass of orange juice
18. A glass of water
19. Nova Scotia smoked salmon on a bagel
20. Poached eggs on toast

5 September

Mined, denim; pools, sloop; slap, pals; star, rats.

9 September

SHIPWRECK

Row, row, row your boat
    Till the prow go down;
Fie on him who borrows sorrow:
All must sink and drown tomorrow;
    All must sink and drown.

Let no wailing crowd your throat;
    Bar your brow from frown;
Bare your breast to Cupid's arrow,
Gnaw the bone and suck the marrow,
    Ere you sink and drown.

Pluck the blossoms life has grown,
    Wear them as a crown;
Many a crow shall fly from sparrow,
Many a lad his row shall harrow
    Ere you sink and drown.

25 September

1. Why not try Betty Crocker's pea soup?
2. Mr. Jones will now play a flute solo.
3. We proudly present the noted news analyst.
4. Come to Tom's restaurant for chicken fricassee.
5. You will know the president has arrived when you hear a twenty-one-gun-salute.
6. Several of the women here tonight are wearing strapless evening gowns.

26 September

Window sign:
Frederic *Chopin* and Johann Sebastian *Bach* were composers.
A *minuet* is a dance.

9 October

There was a young curate of Sarum
Whose manners were quite harum-scarum.
    He ran around Hants
    Without any pants,
Till the vicar compelled him to wear 'em.

A young man called Chumley Coon
Kept as a pet a baboon.
    His mother said, "Chumley,
    Do you think it quite comely
To feed your baboon with a spoon?"

14 October

1. I envy you.
2. Are you sleepy? Yes I am. I am sleepy too.
3. Oh, see the bee! The bee is a busy bee. Oh, yes! The bee is too busy!
4. This is a peony for you.
5. Are you okay? Yes, I am okay, thank you.
6. Are you an animal? I am an Indian, I am in a tepee.
7. Oh, you cutie. You are a beauty.

8. See, the hen has eggs! Yes, I see. The hen has five eggs.
9. I see the seal. The seal is in the sea. I see the deer. The deer is in the ivy.

17 October

The *sober* truth I must relate:
    The queen won't wear her *robes* of state.
It *bores* her when the Royal Guard
    Mistake her for a playing card.

"Dame, say where *Edam* cheese comes from,
    comes from?"
"Cow's milk; I milk them by the sea, the sea."
"And what is *mead made* from, old chum, old chum?"
"Bee's milk; but they aren't milked by me, by me."

22 October

1. The use of drugs is on the increase.
2. If the shoe was on the other foot.
3. I don't pull any punches about it.
4. You're beating around the bush.
5. You are off your rocker.
6. You set my teeth on edge.
7. He will lend an ear to anyone who wants to speak.

23 October

I saw a peacock. With a fiery tail
I saw a blazing comet. Drop down hail
I saw a cloud. Wrapped with ivy round
I saw an oak. Creep on along the ground
I saw a pismire. Swallow up a whale
I saw the sea. Brimful of ale
I saw a Venice glass. Full fathom deep
I saw a well. Full of men's tears that weep
I saw red eyes. All of a flaming fire
I saw a house. Bigger than the moon and higher
I saw the sun. At twelve o'clock at night
I saw the man that saw this wondrous sight.

24 October

(1) Wolf (A*WOL f*or) (2) In (*I n*ever) (3) Sheep's (ban*shee*; *p*shaw) (4) Clothing (terrifi*c lot hing*es). Combined: WOLF IN SHEEP'S CLOTHING.

2 November

(1) Maritime (2) Lawsuit (3) Locomotion (or loco motion) (4) Handicap (5) Stalemate (6) Shamrock

11 November

I voted for the *slate* of candidates
Who, if elected, seemed *least* apt to *steal.*
Now from the *tales* I hear there emanates
The old *stale* story of a double deal.

He *opts* for gold,   He'd beat his wife
As I for ale;   To *spot* a fee.
I've *pots* of this;   Yet, *stop!* I wis
Of that has he.   (And I'd *post* bail)
For me a kiss   He'd pay fourfold
Tops Holy Grail;   To be like me.

17 November

When I was looking out the window, I saw a fire engine; climbing a wall, I saw a swallow; drinking soda, I saw a baby; bigger than a house, I saw the sun; as green as cheese, I saw the grass; drinking beer, I saw two old men as drunk as I.

(Look also at the answer for 23 October.)

18 November

Corner Third and Thirty-third   Along came Myrtle
Thirty dirty purple birds   And her girl friend Gertie.
Sittin' on the curb   Boy, were they perturbed.
Eatin' worms
And chirpin' and burpin'.

20 November

VILE VODKA

Who of vodka distilled from potatoes partakes
    Should take warning:
He'll be jolly at night, but morose when he wakes
    In the morning.

23 November

Wow, Hannah, radar, redder, did, noon, ma'am, Otto, pup, eye

27 November

1. I understand you undertake to overthrow my undertakings.
2. Be above quarrels between man and wife. There are faults on both sides.
3. I am under par.
4. If the grate be (great B) empty, put coal on (colon). If the grate be full, stop putting coal on (colon).

10 December

The words make a round (that is, they go around and end where they began): table tennis, tennis elbow, elbow grease, greasepaint, paintbrush, brush-off, off-white. The one unmatched word is *card.* So the missing word at a Christmas celebration must be *Christmas,* and the round continues: white Christmas, Christmas card, card table, table tennis . . . and so on.

15 December

Why pick a low profession
Like music
That's full of vile practices
Confirmed liars
Old fiddles
And base desires?
. . . For the loot, of course.

16 December

Next week offer me romance.
Hold me; dance and dance and dance.
Answer, answer, answer, do;
Let us turn a pace or two.

20 December

1. Be it ever so humble, there's no place like home.
2. I got up at the crack of dawn.
3. We are all created equal.
4. I refused to tell him who I was—I used a fictitious name.
5. The food in that restaurant is abominable.
6. Explain it to me in words of one syllable.
7. Congress is still in session.
8. All of Abe Lincoln's pictures make him look so thin and emaciated.

Index of Rhetorical Devices and Categories

A

ABBREVIATIONS. 16 May; 20 July.

ABC LANGUAGE. 29 January; 9 March; 14 June; 15 October; 18 December.

ACCIDENTAL ENGLISH. 6 January.

ACRONYMS. 21 May.

ALLITERATION. 3 February.

ANAGRAMS. 29 April; 16 July; 5 September; 17 October; 11 November.

ANGUISH LANGUISH. 3 July; 16 December.

ANIMAL ALPHABET. 11 January.

ANIMALS. 22 January; 24 February; 13 April; 5 May; 5 October; 13 November; 7 December.

B

BACK SLANG. 6 February.

BET YOU DIDN'T KNOW THAT! 24 January; 21 April; 7 September; 14 October; 15 November; 8 December.

BIRTHDAYS. 1, 14 April; 5 August; 18 September; 12 October.

BURIED WORDS. 16 March; 5 July; 24 October.

C

CALLING NAMES. 20 March.

CLERIHEWS. 12 February.

COLLECTIVE NOUNS. 13 February; 19 March.

COUNTING RHYMES. 4 February; 10 March; 15, 29 July; 8 September; 25 October; 12, 20, 30 November; 4, 30 December.

COUNTRY MUSIC. 29 December.

CRAZY GRAMMAR. 16, 20 January; 9 February; 12, 31 March; 7, 26 April; 26 May; 23 June; 28 July; 19 September; 3 October; 14 December.

CRAZY LOGIC. 6 March; 25 June; 29 September; 30 November; 17 December.

CROSSING JOKES. 10 January.

CROSSWORD PUZZLES. 9 April; 6 August.

D

DEAR DEPARTED. 10 April.

DIALECTS. 22 September; 18 November.

E

ENDLESS TALES. 10 November.

EPITAPHS. 12 January; 27 April; 15 June; 17 August.

F

FACTS. 24 January; 21 April; 7 September; 14 October; 15 November; 8 December.

G

GLIMPSES OF GOD. 6 June.

H

HASH-HOUSE LANGUAGE. 4 September.
HOLIDAYS. 14, 22, 29 February; 17 March; 12, 31 October; 31 December.
HOMONYMS. 14 May; 4 August.

I

IMPOSSIBLE RHYMES. 19 May.
IN THE FOREIGN FASHION. 21 January; 10, 15, 26 February; 25 March; 15 April; 20 September; 9 November; 12, 22 December.
IRISH BULLS. 23 April; 16, 31 August.

J

JARGON. 4 June.
JOKES. 11, 27, 30 January; 5 February; 13, 23 March; 24, 28 May; 19, 30 June; 27 July; 2, 10, 26, 28 August; 28 October; 29 November.
JUMBLED GEOGRAPHY. 8 February; 18 July; 11 October; 5 December.

K

KNOCK KNOCKS. 15 January; 28 March; 11 June; 11 September; 3 December.

L

LETTER-ADDS. 21 July; 8 August; 9 September.
LETTER-BY-LETTER. 17 January; 14 March; 2, 15 May.
LIMERICKS. 3, 25 January; 7, 29 March; 11, 25 April; 12, 27 May; 7, 16 June; 10, 26 July; 22, 24 August; 6, 29, September. 19 October; 3 November; 6 December.
LITTLE AUDREY. 11 May; 21 November.
LITTLE MORONS. 17 April; 14 August; 10 October.
LITTLE WILLIES. 14 January; 12 September.
LOGIC, ETC. 26 September.
LONG WORDS. 20 May; 9 July.

M

MALAPROPISMS. 21 February; 13 September; 22 October; 20 December.
MEMORY AIDS. 18 June.
METAPHORS. 2 June.

N

NAMES. 15 March; 27 June; 25 November.
NONSENSE. 18 January; 17 February; 3, 11, 17, 26 March; 3, 28 April; 10, 23, 30 May; 20, 24 June; 13, 17, 24 July; 20, 27, 29 August; 14, 16, 27, September; 7, 16, 27 October; 5, 26 November; 9, 11, 19, 21, 26, 30 December.
NUMBERS FUN. 6, 18 April; 9 June; 13 August; 26 October.

O

ON THE DANGERS OF THINKING. 25 February.
ONOMATOPOEIA. 3 May; 31 July; 3 August.

P

PALINDROMES. 7 February; 13 May; 10 September; 8 October; 23 November.
PANGRAMS. 11 August.
PICTURE POEMS. 5 January; 13 December.
PIG LATIN. 9 August.
PRONUNCIATION. 28 February; 2, 19 April; 10 June; 9 October; 22 November.
PUNCTUATION PUZZLES. 5 March; 17 June; 23 August; 23 October; 17 November.
PUNS. 2, 31 January; 7, 27 May; 28 June; 8 July; 2, 21 October; 2 November; 15 December.
PUZZLES. 10, 27 December.
PUSH BUTTON TUNES. 19 July.

R

REBUSES. 28 January; 4 April; 22 July; 27 November.
RIDDLES. 7 January; 2 February; 8, 21 March; 5, 14, 30 April; 6 May; 3, 21 June; 12, 30 July; 21 September; 4, 30 October; 7 November.

S

THE SEASONS. 24 April; 18 October.
SIMILES. 22 November.
SHIFTY SENTENCES. 19 January.
A SLIP OR TWO. 27 March; 17 May; 13 June; 19 August; 13 October.
SPELLING. 23 January; 18 August.
SPLIT WORDS. 4 March.
SPOONERISMS. 2 March; 29 May; 2 July; 25 September.
STINKY PINKIES. 27 February; 14 July.
STORIES. 26 January; 11, 29 February; 18, 24 March; 16 April; 8 May; 7, 25 July; 7 August; 17 September; 29 October; 2, 25 December.
SUPERSTITIONS. 13 January.
SYMBOLS. 20 April.

T

TOM SWIFTIES. 18 February; 18 May; 21 August.
TONGUE TWISTERS. 20 February; 12 June; 16 November.
TRANSLATION. 4 July.

U

UNKIND CUTS. 12 April.
USAGE. 2 September.

V

VERSES. 1, 4, 8, 11, 22 January; 1, 6, 14, 19, 22 February; 1, 22 March; 1, 24 April; 1 May; 1, 5, 7, 14, 23, 26 June; 1, 6, 18, 20 July; 1, 5, 18 August; 1, 9, 12, 18, 22, 24, 30 September; 1, 5, 11, 12, 18, 31 October; 1, 14, 22, 24, 28 November; 1, 7, 8, 28, 31 December. (See also COUNTING RHYMES, LIMERICKS, NONSENSE.)
VOWELS IN ORDER. 3 September.

W

WHAT QUEER WORDS! 8 June.
WHERE DID THOSE WORDS/ EXPRESSIONS COME FROM? 16, 23 February; 30 March; 8, 22 April; 4, 22, 31 May; 22, 29 June; 11, 23 July; 12, 15, 25, 30 August; 15, 23 September; 6, 20 October; 4, 19 November, 24 December.
WHERE THOSE WORDS DIDN'T COME FROM. 9 January.
WORD GAMES. 9, 25 May; 6 November.
WORD TWINS. 8 January.

hu-ba 10.17(0)